The New Temple Shakespeare

Edited by M. R. RIDLEY, M.A.

SONNETS
by William Shakespeare

6702

J. M. DENT & SONS LTD., London
E. P. DUTTON & CO., INC., New York

Editor's General Note

THE TEXT. The editor has kept before him the aim of presenting to the modern reader the nearest possible approximation to what Shakespeare actually wrote. The text is therefore conservative, and is based on the earliest reliable printed text. But to avoid distraction (*a*) the spelling is modernised, and (*b*) a limited number of universally accepted emendations is admitted without comment. Where a Quarto text exists as well as the First Folio the passages which occur only in the Quarto are enclosed in square brackets [ ] and those which occur only in the Folio in brace brackets { }.

SCENE DIVISION. The rapid continuity of the Elizabethan curtainless production is lost by the 'traditional' scene divisions. Where there is an essential difference of place these scene divisions are retained. Where on the other hand the change of place is insignificant the scene division is indicated only by a space on the page. For ease of reference, however, the 'traditional' division is retained at the head of the page and in line numbering.

NOTES. Passages on which there are notes are indicated by a † in the margin.

PUNCTUATION adheres more closely than has been usual to the 'Elizabethan' punctuation of the early texts. It is often therefore more indicative of the way in which the lines were to be delivered than of their syntactical construction.

vii

SONNETS

GLOSSARIES are arranged on a somewhat novel princi-
ple, not alphabetically, but in the order in which the
words or phrases occur. The editor is much indebted to
Mr. J. N. Bryson for his collaboration in the preparation
of the glossaries.

Preface

THE TEXT. The Sonnets were entered in the Stationers' Registers in May of 1609 and published in that year, with the following title-page. "SHAKE-SPEARES / SONNETS. / Neuer before Imprinted. / AT LONDON / By *G. Eld* for *T. T.* and are / to be solde by *Iohn Wright*, dwelling / at Christ Church gate. / 1609." or in some copies "to be solde by *William Aspley*." The sonnets are on the whole well printed. There was no other edition until 1640, when "Poems: written by Wil. Shakespeare, Gent" appeared. This included the bulk of the sonnets, omitting eight of them and rearranging the others under various titles. This edition is of no value for the determination of the text, but it has some interest as showing that thirty-one years after their original publication the order of the sonnets in the 1609 edition was not regarded as sacrosanct.

PROBLEMS OF THE SONNETS. The sonnets present various problems which have, perhaps more than was need, vexed the critics, who have in turn transferred their vexations to the reader, making it, so far as such an unwished consummation could be achieved, impossible to read the sonnets just as great poetry. The main problems are these:—1. Are the sonnets a record of actual experience, or are they 'dramatic' and imaginary? 2. If they are a record of experience, (*a*) to whom were they addressed? (*i.e.* who was Mr. W. H.?); (*b*) who was the rival poet?

(c) who was the dark lady? 3. Are the sonnets a 'sequence' and, if so, what is their proper order? 4. When were they written?

1. Particular sonnets, taken in isolation, will support either view. Any reader who does not feel that the famous 'Lust in action' sonnet is written from experience, as direct and bitter as that, *e.g.* of Burns, is, one may think, past praying for; but the two sonnets on Cupid and his brand are merely two conventional exercises on the same conventional theme. Moreover, the temptation to think that here at least we have the otherwise inscrutable dramatist speaking in his own voice as the poet is almost irresistible, and should be allowed for in forming our judgment. And we must at least reckon with the possibility that what we have here is neither a direct record of actual experience, nor yet something purely imaginary and conventional, but a number of pieces of work in a conventional form, to vitalise which, and raise them above the merely conventional, Shakespeare drew, as in his dramas, upon his own experience. But the general instinct of readers, and I believe the just instinct, has been to feel that in the sonnets we have, at any rate in large measure, the record of Shakespeare's own intimate personal experience.

2. (a) To whom were the sonnets addressed? The arena is mainly occupied by the rival parties of the Herbertists and the Southamptonites, and the contest is from time to time enlivened and confused by the incursions of guerrilla supporters of less well known claimants, such as William Hughes, William Hathaway, or 'William Himself.' The contest is an entertaining spectacle, but the activities of the contestants seem about as practically useful, in helping our understanding or appreciation of the sonnets, as those of the traditional blind man on a

dark night looking for a black cat that is not there. If we knew that there were only two possible claimants, that Mr. W. H. was either William Herbert, Earl of Pembroke, or Henry Wriothesley, Earl of Southampton, there would be a straight issue, and the problem would be worth pursuing. But we know nothing of the kind. We are looking for a young man, probably of noble birth, whose initials may or may not have been W. H., to whom Shakespeare was passionately attached, whose mother was beautiful, whose father was probably, but by no means certainly, dead, who showed a certain reluctance to get married, but no reluctance at all to supplant Shakespeare in the affections of a dark lady. The main battle is, not unnaturally, something of a stalemate. The Southamptonites point to the undoubted facts that Southampton was Shakespeare's patron, that *Venus and Adonis* and *Lucrece* are both dedicated to him, the second in words which resemble those of one of the sonnets, and that his father died when he was a boy; and they get over the trouble of his initials, and of the 'Will' sonnets, as best they can. The Herbertists retort that this is all very well, but that, apart from the unfortunate fact that he was called Henry, so far from showing any reluctance to get married he got into serious trouble with the Queen for wanting to marry Elizabeth Vernon in 1595, and married her whether or no in 1598; whereas their man was averse from marriage, but had a liaison with Mary Fitton, who will do very well for the dark lady, that he was called William, that his initials are W. H., and that on the evidence of Heminge and Condell he treated Shakespeare with favour. The other party then reasonably point out that as Pembroke did not come to London till 1598, either the sonnets must have been written with very remarkable rapidity, or else Meres's comments in the same year on the 'sugred sonnets' must refer to some others. And so on, and so on.

Where the field of conjecture is so wide, and the criteria by which to estimate evidence so uncertain, any attempt to summarise the conflicting arguments would be, I think, as idle as, within the limits of this preface, it would be impossible.

(*b*) Who was the rival poet? This is at least a more reasonable question. The number of Elizabethan poets who could have merited Shakespeare's description is at least very much smaller than that of the young noblemen, known or unknown, who might have had the necessary qualifications. Of the various possibilities Chapman appears the most probable, and the probability is increased if we agree that there is a good deal of allusion to Chapman in *Love's Labour's Lost*, between which and the sonnets there are very obvious connections.

(*c*) Who was the dark lady? Here again the field of conjecture is far too wide for any certainty to have been attained, or indeed to be attainable. But that, whatever her name was, she existed, and that Shakespeare loved her, can hardly be doubted by anyone who reads the 'dark lady' sonnets and reads also some of the speeches of Berowne in *Love's Labour's Lost*.

3. What is the proper order of the sonnets? If we are to consider this question at all we must start with the assumption that the sonnets did at one time form a sequence, or two sequences, or at least fell into recognisable groups. If they did not, *cadit quæstio*, and we can read the sonnets in any order we choose. It has, however, been universally recognised that the sonnets, whether or not they form a sequence, do fall into two main groups, those addressed to the friend, and those addressed to the dark lady. It is also clear that there is a number of pairs of sonnets, the members of which, if separated, either become almost meaningless or at best

lose much of their force. Further, there seem to be some-what larger groups of half a dozen or so sonnets which might be distinguished by arbitrary titles such as 'Night thoughts,' 'Love in absence,' and so on. And on the whole most readers, I suppose, have the feeling that the sonnets, or the bulk of them, were intended to form a sonnet sequence, whether or not the order of the 1609 edition represents the intention correctly. (It is further to be noticed, though this is a matter merely of grammar, and has nothing to do with subject-matter, that some of the sonnets adhere to 'thou,' 'thee,' etc., for the second person of address, while others adhere to 'you' and 'your,' a dif-ference which is presumably significant of something.) Now few editors (Dowden being a notable and heroic exception), and probably fewer readers, have ever been wholly satisfied with the order of 1609. The game of rearrangement began in 1640 and has been carried on ever since. It is, very naturally, a tempting game to play. Every reader must, for example, have been struck by the awkward abruptness of the opening. Before we have any indication of the relations between Shakespeare and the man he is addressing we are plunged straight, in the 1609 edition, into exhortations to marry. And I suppose that every reader who has read the sonnets with more than the most casual attention has perpetually found himself saying to himself, "But this sonnet is surely connected with that other, ten pages back." But the game is just as unsatisfactory as it is tempting, because all rearrange-ments were governed, and till recently it appeared as though they must always be governed, by nothing more secure than the personal idiosyncrasy and insight of the individual editor or reader. As a result the more con-servative editors, unwilling to leave a harbour, however inconvenient, for an uncharted sea on which they were going to have no compass other than one which they were modest enough to distrust, namely their own taste, have tended to adhere to the 1609 order, either defending it with Dowden, or permitting themselves no more than an occasional suggestion, such as those of Mr. Knox Pooler, "Perhaps out of place" or "Perhaps this sonnet should be grouped with those that express world-weariness." But before we acquiesce in remaining in harbour, we are wise to ask ourselves what kind of harbour it is. And here, it seems to me, there are only two alternatives. Either the 1609 order is Shakespeare's own, and then there is no more to be said, or else it is not, and then it has exactly as much or as little authority as any other order of any date. And the moment that we accept the second alternative, and emancipate ourselves from the notion that the 1609 order, merely because it is old, has some vague superiority of antiquity over later arrangements, we begin to wonder insistently whether we cannot somewhere find a more reliable compass, one that will, like proper compasses, work whether we like it or not.

Sir Denys Bray was, so far as I know, the first to point out, in 1925, that there is one possible test of the order in which the sonnets may be arranged which is perfectly mechanical, which can be rigidly applied by anyone irrespective of his taste, and the application of which produces some highly interesting results. This test consists of the 'rhyme-link,' which is in fact present in the pairs of sonnets which no rearrangement has ever separated, and which, with a particular rearrangement, can be seen linking all the sonnets in a continuous chain. There is no space here even to summarise the details of the application of the method. They must be studied in Sir Denys Bray's own book.[1] It is enough perhaps to say that the permuta-

[1] *The Original Order of Shakespeare's Sonnets,* Sir Denys Bray: Methuen, 1925 (see also his "The Art-form of the Elizabethan Sonnet Sequence and Shakespeare's Sonnets" in the *Shakespeare-Jahrbuch,* 1927).

tions which turn out to be possible if the link is adhered to
are found to be in practice very much more strictly limited than one's expectation suggests, and then to point out
certain striking features which the order so arrived at
presents. In the first place, if the new arrangement was
going to disintegrate even a few of the pairs of sonnets
which have been universally recognised as connected,
one would probably reject it out of hand, and if this order
were merely accidental it would be almost inevitable that
at least one or two of the pairs would be split. In fact, of
the eighteen such pairs (I–II, V–VI, IX–X, XV–XVI,
XXXIII–XXXIV, XLIV–XLV, XLVI–XLVII, L–LI,
LXIX–LXX, LXXIII–LXXIV, LXXIX–LXXX, LXXXVIII–
LXXXIX, XCV–XCVI, CXIII–CXIV, CXVI–CXVII,
CXVIII–CXIX, CXXXIII–CXXXIV, CXLVII–CXLVIII),
and the one such triplet (LXXXIV–VI), all without exception are left undisturbed. And these compose just
over a quarter of the total number of sonnets. In the
second place, many of the conjectures of even conservative editors receive confirmation. When, for example, we
find Mr. Knox Pooler saying that XXIV perhaps precedes
XLVI, that XXVII is perhaps continued in XLIII, of which
either XXIV, XXVIII or LXI is perhaps the continuation,
and then turn to the rhyme-linked order, and find that in
a small group of fourteen sonnets the first two are
XXIV and XLVI, and the last four XXVII, XLIII, LXI,
and XXVIII, our natural scepticism begins to be a trifle
shaken. When we find him further saying of LII 'perhaps
a continuation of XLVIII,' of LXXV 'cf. XLVIII, XLIX,'
of CVI 'cf. LIX,' of CXXII 'cf. LXXVII,' and find in the
rhyme-linked order LXXV–LII–XLVIII, CVI–LIX, and
LXXVII–CXXII; and when further we find that in the
'dark lady' series six notes of 'compare' or 'this seems to
be connected with' are confirmed by the rhyme-link, not

to mention the fact that the 'will' sonnet, CXLIII, finds its natural place next to the other two 'will' sonnets, CXXXV and CXXXVI, scepticism receives a further blow, and we begin to feel, I think, at least this, that the rhyme-link appears to be producing a much more interesting and coherent order out of chaos. (For what it is worth the present editor's own scepticism received a rude shock when among some casual notes of his own on the sonnets, made without any reference to Sir Denys Bray's book, he found an entry "XXXIII–XXXV, XL, and XCV, XCVI look as though they belonged to one group of 'Reproaches,'" and then found in the linked order, in a group of fourteen sonnets, XXXIII, XXXIV, XL, XCV and XCVI, as five of the first six and XXXV later in the same group.) One further point should be mentioned, which is perhaps from the mechanical standpoint the most remarkable of all. If from the linked order one abstracts all the 'you' sonnets, the 'thou' sonnets still remain linked, a significant oddity which seems to be beyond the reach of chance.

I wish to claim for Sir Denys Bray's order no more than this, that by the application of a perfectly mechanical criterion, which is in no way dependent on the idiosyncrasies of any editor, an order of the sonnets is produced which makes them a far more coherent and readable series than the order of 1609. And even if the production of that order were a mere accident, which I find it difficult to believe, we might well be grateful for an accident which so much enhances our pleasure. The sonnets are therefore here given in the 'linked' order, the traditional numbering being given, for ease of reference, in Roman numerals in brackets.

4. When were the sonnets written? Shakespeare speaks in 1593 of *Venus and Adonis* as the first heir of his invention; Meres in 1598 speaks of Shakespeare's 'sugred

sonnets'; two of the sonnets were incorporated in *The Passionate Pilgrim* in 1599. That implies that all the sonnets are later than 1593, and that some of them are earlier than 1598. That is all the direct evidence that we have. From parallels between passages in the sonnets and passages in the plays, from supposed references in the sonnets to historical events, and from uncertain allusions to events in the life of Herbert (if we are Herbertists) or Southampton (if we belong to that camp) or of 'William Himself,' we can draw such further conclusions as we please. And there is some reason to guess that the 'you' sonnets are separated in date by some interval from the 'thou' sonnets. But the grounds of conjecture are far too insecure, and the profit of it far too inconsiderable, to allure us for long.

I have inserted no 'analysis' or 'table of contents' of the sonnets. Such an analysis involves the breaking of them up into groups, and the invention of titles for the groups. And though they do no doubt fall into groups, I think that most readers will prefer to follow the clear progress and shift of the thought without the editor's officious aid. For the same reason the notes are reduced to a minimum, and consist largely of parallel passages from the plays. There are very few passages in the sonnets which suggest textual corruption; there are, on the other hand, a great many which do not yield their meaning on a first reading. But as the only method of elucidation is a more or less clumsy paraphrase, a method even less tolerable in dealing with the 'pure' poetry of the sonnets than in dealing with the 'dramatic' poetry of the plays, and as all that is needed for almost all these passages is a little patience and imagination, I think that most readers will prefer their own interpretations to mine.

SONNETS

The list below gives the numbering of the Sonnets in the 1609 edition (in Roman numerals) and of this edition (in Arabic); the former also appear at the foot of each Sonnet:

I	15	XXXI	4	LXI	40	XCI	2
II	16	XXXII	47	LXII	6	XCII	72
III	24	XXXIII	66	LXIII	85	XCIII	74
IV	17	XXXIV	67	LXIV	120	XCIV	117
V	21	XXXV	78	LXV	10	XCV	70
VI	22	XXXVI	114	LXVI	45	XCVI	71
VII	27	XXXVII	121	LXVII	64	XCVII	80
VIII	23	XXXVIII	58	LXVIII	87	XCVIII	82
IX	18	XXXIX	113	LXIX	63	XCIX	89
X	19	XL	69	LXX	62	C	84
XI	14	XLI	79	LXXI	46	CI	55
XII	26	XLII	68	LXXII	48	CII	83
XIII	13	XLIII	39	LXXIII	42	CIII	49
XIV	20	XLIV	36	LXXIV	43	CIV	88
XV	11	XLV	37	LXXV	31	CV	57
XVI	12	XLVI	29	LXXVI	93	CVI	99
XVII	25	XLVII	30	LXXVII	90	CVII	97
XVIII	8	XLVIII	33	LXXVIII	59	CVIII	101
XIX	86	XLIX	104	LXXIX	54	CIX	108
XX	1	L	34	LXXX	53	CX	122
XXI	61	LI	35	LXXXI	44	CXI	118
XXII	7	LII	32	LXXXII	60	CXII	112
XXIII	103	LIII	5	LXXXIII	56	CXIII	105
XXIV	28	LIV	65	LXXXIV	50	CXIV	106
XXV	3	LV	98	LXXXV	51	CXV	95
XXVI	102	LVI	81	LXXXVI	52	CXVI	110
XXVII	38	LVII	73	LXXXVII	126	CXVII	109
XXVIII	41	LVIII	75	LXXXVIII	76	CXVIII	124
XXIX	125	LIX	100	LXXXIX	77	CXIX	123
XXX	116	LX	119	XC	115	CXX	111

SONNETS

TO . THE . ONLIE . BEGETTER . OF .

THESE . INSVING . SONNETS .

M^R. W. H. ALL . HAPPINESSE .

AND . THAT . ETERNITIE .

PROMISED .

BY .

OVR . EVER-LIVING . POET .

WISHETH .

THE . WELL-WISHING .

ADVENTVRER . IN .

SETTING .

FORTH .

T. T.

1

A woman's face with Nature's own hand painted
Hast thou, the master-mistress of my passion,
A woman's gentle heart, but not acquainted
With shifting change, as is false women's fashion,
An eye more bright than theirs, less false in rolling,
Gilding the object whereupon it gazeth;
A man in hue, all hues in his controlling,   †
Which steals men's eyes and women's souls amazeth.
And for a woman wert thou first created;
Till Nature as she wrought thee fell a-doting,
And by addition me of thee defeated,
By adding one thing to my purpose nothing.
   But since she prick'd thee out for women's pleasure,
   Mine be thy love, and thy love's use their treasure.

[xx]

2

Some glory in their birth, some in their skill,
Some in their wealth, some in their body's force,
Some in their garments though new-fangled ill,
Some in their hawks and hounds, some in their horse;
And every humour hath his adjunct pleasure,
Wherein it finds a joy above the rest,
But these particulars are not my measure;
All these I better in one general best.
Thy love is better than high birth to me,
Richer than wealth, prouder than garments' cost,   †
Of more delight than hawks or horses be;
And having thee, of all men's pride I boast:
   Wretched in this alone, that thou mayst take
   All this away, and me most wretched make.

[xci]

3

Let those who are in favour with their stars
Of public honour and proud titles boast,
Whilst I, whom fortune of such triumph bars,
Unlook'd for joy in that I honour most;
Great princes' favourites their fair leaves spread
But as the marigold at the sun's eye,
And in themselves their pride lies buried,
For at a frown they in their glory die.
The painful warrior famoused for worth,   †
After a thousand victories once foil'd,
Is from the book of honour razed forth,
And all the rest forgot for which he toil'd:
 Then happy I, that love and am beloved
 Where I may not remove, nor be removed.

[xxv]

4

Thy bosom is endeared with all hearts,
Which I by lacking have supposed dead;
And there reigns love, and all love's loving parts,
And all those friends which I thought buried.
How many a holy and obsequious tear
Hath dear religious love stol'n from mine eye,
As interest of the dead, which now appear
But things remov'd that hidden in thee lie!
Thou art the grave where buried love doth live,
Hung with the trophies of my lovers gone,
Who all their parts of me to thee did give,
That due of many now is thine alone:
 Their images I lov'd I view in thee,
 And thou (all they) hast all the all of me.

[xxxi]

5

What is your substance, whereof are you made,
That millions of strange shadows on you tend?
Since every one hath, every one, one shade,
And you, but one, can every shadow lend.
Describe Adonis, and the counterfeit
Is poorly imitated after you;
On Helen's cheek all art of beauty set,
And you in Grecian tires are painted new:
Speak of the spring and foison of the year,
The one doth shadow of your beauty show,
The other as your bounty doth appear,
And you in every blessed shape we know.
　　In all external grace you have some part,
　　But you like none, none you, for constant heart.

[LIII]

6

Sin of self-love possesseth all mine eye,
And all my soul, and all my every part;
And for this sin there is no remedy,
It is so grounded inward in my heart.
Methinks no face so gracious is as mine,
No shape so true, no truth of such account;
And for myself mine own worth do define,　　†
As I all other in all worths surmount.
But when my glass shows me myself indeed,
Beated and chopp'd with tann'd antiquity,
Mine own self-love quite contrary I read;
Self so self-loving were iniquity.
　　'Tis thee (myself) that for myself I praise
　　Painting my age with beauty of thy days.

[LXII]

3

7

My glass shall not persuade me I am old,
So long as youth and thou are of one date,
But when in thee time's furrows I behold,
Then look I death my days should expiate.   †
For all that beauty that doth cover thee
Is but the seemly raiment of my heart,
Which in thy breast doth live, as thine in me;
How can I then be elder than thou art?
O, therefore, love, be of thyself so wary
As I, not for myself, but for thee will,
Bearing thy heart, which I will keep so chary
As tender nurse her babe from faring ill.
    Presume not on thy heart when mine is slain;
    Thou gav'st me thine not to give back again.

[xxii]

8

Shall I compare thee to a summer's day?
Thou art more lovely and more temperate:
Rough winds do shake the darling buds of May,
And summer's lease hath all too short a date:
Sometime too hot the eye of heaven shines,
And often is his gold complexion dimm'd,
And every fair from fair sometime declines,
By chance, or nature's changing course, untrimm'd;
But thy eternal summer shall not fade,
Nor lose possession of that fair thou ow'st;
Nor shall Death brag thou wander'st in his shade,
When in eternal lines to time thou grow'st:
    So long as men can breathe, or eyes can see,
    So long lives this, and this gives life to thee.

[xviii]

9

                                         †

O thou, my lovely boy, who in thy power
Dost hold Time's fickle glass, his sickle, hour;   †
Who hast by waning grown, and therein show'st
Thy lovers withering, as thy sweet self grow'st;
If Nature, sovereign mistress over wrack,
As thou goest onwards, still will pluck thee back,
She keeps thee to this purpose, that her skill
May time disgrace and wretched minutes kill.
Yet fear her, O thou minion of her pleasure!
She may detain, but not still keep, her treasure:
Her audit (though delay'd) answer'd must be,
And her quietus is to render thee.

                                       [CXXVI]

10

Since brass, nor stone, nor earth, nor boundless sea,
But sad mortality o'er-sways their power,
How with this rage shall beauty hold a plea,
Whose action is no stronger than a flower?
O, how shall summer's honey breath hold out
Against the wreckful siege of battering days,
When rocks impregnable are not so stout,
Nor gates of steel so strong, but Time decays?
O fearful meditation! where, alack,
Shall Time's best jewel from Time's chest lie hid?
Or what strong hand can hold his swift foot back,
Or who his spoil of beauty can forbid?
    O, none, unless this miracle have might,
    That in black ink my love may still shine bright.

                                         [LXV]

11

When I consider every thing that grows
Holds in perfection but a little moment,
That this huge stage presenteth nought but shows
Whereon the stars in secret influence comment;
When I perceive that men as plants increase,
Cheered and check'd even by the self-same sky,
Vaunt in their youthful sap, at height decrease,
And wear their brave state out of memory;
Then the conceit of this inconstant stay
Sets you most rich in youth before my sight,
Where wasteful Time debateth with Decay,
To change your day of youth to sullied night;
    And all in war with Time for love of you,
    As he takes from you, I engraft you new.

[xv]

12

But wherefore do not you a mightier way
Make war upon this bloody tyrant Time?
And fortify yourself in your decay
With means more blessed than my barren rhyme?
Now stand you on the top of happy hours,
And many maiden gardens, yet unset,
With virtuous wish would bear your living flowers,
Much liker than your painted counterfeit:
So should the lines of life that life repair,
Which this (Time's pencil or my pupil pen)   †
Neither in inward worth nor outward fair,
Can make you live yourself in eyes of men.
    To give away yourself keeps yourself still;
    And you must live, drawn by your own sweet skill.

[xvi]

13

O, that you were yourself! but, love, you are   †
No longer yours than you yourself here live:
Against this coming end you should prepare,
And your sweet semblance to some other give.
So should that beauty which you hold in lease
Find no determination; then you were
Yourself again after yourself's decease,
When your sweet issue your sweet form should bear.
Who lets so fair a house fall to decay,
Which husbandry in honour might uphold
Against the stormy gusts of winter's day
And barren rage of death's eternal cold?
   O, none but unthrifts, dear my love you know,   †
   You had a father, let your son say so.

[xiii]

14

As fast as thou shalt wane, so fast thou grow'st
In one of thine, from that which thou departest,
And that fresh blood, which youngly thou bestow'st,
Thou mayst call thine, when thou from youth convertest.
Herein lives wisdom, beauty, and increase,
Without this, folly, age, and cold decay;
If all were minded so, the times should cease,
And threescore year would make the world away:
Let those whom Nature hath not made for store,
Harsh, featureless, and rude, barrenly perish:
Look, whom she best endow'd she gave the more;
Which bounteous gift thou shouldst in bounty cherish:
   She carv'd thee for her seal, and meant thereby
   Thou shouldst print more, not let that copy die.

[xi]

15

From fairest creatures we desire increase,
That thereby beauty's rose might never die,
But as the riper should by time decease,
His tender heir might bear his memory:
But thou, contracted to thine own bright eyes,
Feed'st thy light's flame with self-substantial fuel,
Making a famine where abundance lies,
Thyself thy foe, to thy sweet self too cruel:
Thou that art now the world's fresh ornament,
And only herald to the gaudy spring,
Within thine own bud buriest thy content,
And, tender churl, mak'st waste in niggarding: †
   Pity the world, or else this glutton be,
   To eat the world's due by the grave and thee.

[I]

16

When forty winters shall besiege thy brow,
And dig deep trenches in thy beauty's field,   †
Thy youth's proud livery, so gaz'd on now,
Will be a tatter'd weed of small worth held:
Then being ask'd where all thy beauty lies,
Where all the treasure of thy lusty days;
To say, within thine own deep-sunken eyes,
Were an ill-eating shame, and thriftless praise.
How much more praise deserv'd thy beauty's use,
If thou couldst answer 'This fair child of mine
Shall sum my count, and make my old excuse,'
Proving his beauty by succession thine!
   This were to be new made when thou art old,
   And see thy blood warm when thou feel'st it cold.

[II]

17

Unthrifty loveliness, why dost thou spend
Upon thyself thy beauty's legacy?
Nature's bequest gives nothing, but doth lend,
And being frank, she lends to those are free:
Then, beauteous niggard, why dost thou abuse
The bounteous largess given thee to give?
Profitless usurer, why dost thou use
So great a sum of sums, yet canst not live?
For having traffic with thyself alone,
Thou of thyself thy sweet self dost deceive;
Then how, when nature calls thee to be gone,
What acceptable audit canst thou leave?
  Thy unus'd beauty must be tomb'd with thee,
  Which, used, lives th' executor to be.

[IV]

18

Is it for fear to wet a widow's eye
That thou consum'st thyself in single life?
Ah! if thou issueless shalt hap to die,
The world will wail thee like a makeless wife,
The world will be thy widow, and still weep
That thou no form of thee hast left behind,
When every private widow well may keep,
By children's eyes, her husband's shape in mind:
Look, what an unthrift in the world doth spend
Shifts but his place, for still the world enjoys it,
But beauty's waste hath in the world an end,
And kept unus'd, the user so destroys it:
  No love toward others in that bosom sits
  That on himself such murderous shame commits.

[IX]

19

For shame deny that thou bear'st love to any
Who for thyself art so unprovident;
Grant, if thou wilt, thou art belov'd of many,
But that thou none lov'st is most evident:
For thou art so possess'd with murderous hate,
That 'gainst thyself thou stick'st not to conspire,
Seeking that beauteous roof to ruinate   †
Which to repair should be thy chief desire:
O change thy thought, that I may change my mind!
Shall hate be fairer lodg'd than gentle love?
Be as thy presence is, gracious and kind,
Or to thyself at least kind-hearted prove,
   Make thee another self, for love of me,
   That beauty still may live in thine or thee.

[x]

20

Not from the stars do I my judgement pluck,
And yet methinks I have astronomy,
But not to tell of good or evil luck,
Of plagues, of dearths, or seasons' quality;
Nor can I fortune to brief minutes tell,
Pointing to each his thunder, rain and wind,
Or say with princes if it shall go well,
By oft predict that I in heaven find:
But from thine eyes my knowledge I derive,   †
And, constant stars, in them I read such art,
As, 'truth and beauty shall together thrive,   †
If from thyself to store thou wouldst convert;'
   Or else of thee this I prognosticate,
   'Thy end is truth's and beauty's doom and date.'

[xiv]

21

Those hours that with gentle work did frame
The lovely gaze, where every eye doth dwell,
Will play the tyrants to the very same,
And that unfair which fairly doth excel:
For never-resting time leads summer on
To hideous winter and confounds him there,
Sap check'd with frost and lusty leaves quite gone,
Beauty o'ersnow'd and bareness every where:
Then, were not summer's distillation left
A liquid prisoner pent in walls of glass,
Beauty's effect with beauty were bereft,
Nor it nor no remembrance what it was: †
  But flowers distill'd, though they with winter meet,
  Leese but their show, their substance still lives sweet.

[v]

22

Then let not winter's ragged hand deface
In thee thy summer ere thou be distill'd:
Make sweet some vial; treasure thou some place
With beauty's treasure, ere it be self-kill'd:
That use is not forbidden usury,
Which happies those that pay the willing loan;
That's for thyself to breed another thee,
Or ten times happier, be it ten for one;
Ten times thyself were happier than thou art,
If ten of thine ten times refigur'd thee,
Then what could death do, if thou shouldst depart,
Leaving thee living in posterity?
  Be not self-will'd, for thou art much too fair
  To be death's conquest and make worms thine heir.

[vi]

23

Music to hear, why hear'st thou music sadly?
Sweets with sweets war not, joy delights in joy:
Why lov'st thou that which thou receiv'st not gladly,
Or else receiv'st with pleasure thine annoy?
If the true concord of well tuned sounds,
By unions married, do offend thine ear,
They do but sweetly chide thee, who confounds
In singleness the parts that thou shouldst bear: †
Mark how one string, sweet husband to another,
Strikes each in each by mutual ordering;
Resembling sire, and child, and happy mother,
Who, all in one, one pleasing note do sing:
 Whose speechless song, being many, seeming one,
 Sings this to thee: 'Thou single wilt prove none.' †

            [viii]

24

Look in thy glass and tell the face thou viewest,
Now is the time that face should form another,
Whose fresh repair if now thou not renewest,
Thou dost beguile the world, unbless some mother.
For where is she so fair whose unear'd womb †
Disdains the tillage of thy husbandry?
Or who is he so fond will be the tomb
Of his self-love, to stop posterity?
Thou art thy mother's glass, and she in thee
Calls back the lovely April of her prime,
So thou through windows of thine age shalt see,
Despite of wrinkles, this thy golden time.
 But if thou live, remember'd not to be,
 Die single, and thine image dies with thee.

            [iii]

25

Who will believe my verse in time to come,
If it were fill'd with your most high deserts?
Though yet heaven knows it is but as a tomb
Which hides your life, and shows not half your parts:
If I could write the beauty of your eyes,
And in fresh numbers number all your graces,
The age to come would say 'This poet lies,
Such heavenly touches ne'er touch'd earthly faces.'
So should my papers (yellowed with their age)
Be scorn'd, like old men of less truth than tongue,
And your true rights be term'd a poet's rage,
And stretched metre of an antique song: †
    But were some child of yours alive that time,
    You should live twice, in it, and in my rhyme.

[xvii]

26

When I do count the clock that tells the time,
And see the brave day sunk in hideous night,
When I behold the violet past prime,
And sable curls all silver'd o'er with white;   †
When lofty trees I see barren of leaves,
Which erst from heat did canopy the herd,
And summer's green all girded up in sheaves,
Borne on the bier with white and bristly beard;
Then of thy beauty do I question make,
That thou among the wastes of time must go,
Since sweets and beauties do themselves forsake,
And die as fast as they see others grow,
    And nothing 'gainst Time's scythe can make defence
    Save breed to brave him, when he takes thee hence.

[xii]

27

Lo, in the orient when the gracious light
Lifts up his burning head, each under eye
Doth homage to his new-appearing sight,
Serving with looks his sacred majesty,
And having climb'd the steep-up heavenly hill,   †
Resembling strong youth in his middle age,
Yet mortal looks adore his beauty still,
Attending on his golden pilgrimage:
But when from highmost pitch, with weary car,
Like feeble age he reeleth from the day,   †
The eyes ('fore duteous) now converted are
From his low tract and look another way:
   So thou, thyself out-going in thy noon,
   Unlook'd on diest unless thou get a son.

[vii]

28

Mine eye hath play'd the painter and hath steel'd   †
Thy beauty's form in table of my heart,
My body is the frame wherein 'tis held,
And perspective it is best painter's art.
For through the painter must you see his skill,
To find where your true image pictur'd lies,
Which in my bosom's shop is hanging still,
That hath his windows glazed with thine eyes.
Now see what good turns eyes for eyes have done;
Mine eyes have drawn thy shape, and thine for me
Are windows to my breast, where-through the sun
Delights to peep, to gaze therein on thee;
   Yet eyes this cunning want to grace their art,
   They draw but what they see, know not the heart.

[xxiv]

29

Mine eye and heart are at a mortal war,
How to divide the conquest of thy sight;
Mine eye my heart thy picture's sight would bar,
My heart mine eye the freedom of that right.
My heart doth plead that thou in him dost lie,
(A closet never pierc'd with crystal eyes)
But the defendant doth that plea deny,
And says in him thy fair appearance lies.
To 'cide this title is impanneled
A quest of thoughts, all tenants to the heart,
And by their verdict is determined
The clear eye's moiety, and the dear heart's part:
  As thus; mine eye's due is thine outward part,
  And my heart's right thine inward love of heart.

[XLVI]

30

Betwixt mine eye and heart a league is took,
And each doth good turns now unto the other,
When that mine eye is famish'd for a look,
Or heart in love with sighs himself doth smother;
With my love's picture then my eye doth feast,
And to the painted banquet bids my heart;
Another time mine eye is my heart's guest,
And in his thoughts of love doth share a part:
So, either by thy picture or my love,
Thyself away are present still with me;
For thou not farther than my thoughts canst move,
And I am still with them, and they with thee;
  Or, if they sleep, thy picture in my sight
  Awakes my heart, to heart's and eye's delight.

[XLVII]

31

So are you to my thoughts as food to life,
Or as sweet-season'd showers are to the ground;
And for the peace of you I hold such strife
As 'twixt a miser and his wealth is found;
Now proud as an enjoyer, and anon
Doubting the filching age will steal his treasure,
Now counting best to be with you alone,
Then better'd that the world may see my pleasure:
Sometime all full with feasting on your sight,
And by and by clean starved for a look,
Possessing or pursuing no delight
Save what is had, or must from you be took.
   Thus do I pine and surfeit day by day,
    Or gluttoning on all, or all away.

[LXXV]

32

So am I as the rich, whose blessed key
Can bring him to his sweet up-locked treasure,
The which he will not every hour survey,
For blunting the fine point of seldom pleasure.
Therefore are feasts so solemn and so rare,
Since, seldom coming, in the long year set,
Like stones of worth they thinly placed are,
Or captain jewels in the carcanet.
So is the time that keeps you as my chest,
Or as the wardrobe which the robe doth hide,
To make some special instant special blest,
By new unfolding his imprison'd pride.
   Blessed are you, whose worthiness gives scope,
    Being had to triumph, being lack'd to hope.

[LII]

33

How careful was I, when I took my way,
Each trifle under truest bars to thrust,
That to my use it might unused stay
From hands of falsehood, in sure wards of trust!
But thou, to whom my jewels trifles are,
Most worthy comfort, now my greatest grief,
Thou best of dearest, and mine only care,
Art left the prey of every vulgar thief.
Thee have I not lock'd up in any chest,
Save where thou art not, though I feel thou art,
Within the gentle closure of my breast,
From whence at pleasure thou mayst come and part;
   And even thence thou wilt be stol'n, I fear,
   For truth proves thievish for a prize so dear.

[XLVIII]

34

How heavy do I journey on the way,
When what I seek (my weary travel's end)
Doth teach that ease and that repose to say,
'Thus far the miles are measur'd from thy friend!'
The beast that bears me, tired with my woe,
Plods duly on, to bear that weight in me,   †
As if by some instinct the wretch did know
His rider lov'd not speed being made from thee:
The bloody spur cannot provoke him on
That sometimes anger thrusts into his hide,
Which heavily he answers with a groan,
More sharp to me than spurring to his side,
   For that same groan doth put this in my mind,
   My grief lies onward and my joy behind.

[L]

35

Thus can my love excuse the slow offence
Of my dull bearer, when from thee I speed;
From where thou art why should I haste me thence?
Till I return, of posting is no need.
O, what excuse will my poor beast then find,
When swift extremity can seem but slow?
Then should I spur though mounted on the wind,
In winged speed no motion shall I know;
Then can no horse with my desire keep pace,
Therefore desire (of perfect'st love being made)
Shall neigh—no dull flesh—in his fiery race,   †
But love, for love, thus shall excuse my jade;
   Since from thee going he went wilful-slow,
   Towards thee I'll run, and give him leave to go.

[LI]

36

If the dull substance of my flesh were thought,
Injurious distance should not stop my way,
For then despite of space I would be brought,
From limits far remote, where thou dost stay;
No matter then although my foot did stand
Upon the farthest earth remov'd from thee,
For nimble thought can jump both sea and land,
As soon as think the place where he would be.
But, ah, thought kills me that I am not thought,
To leap large lengths of miles when thou art gone,
But that, so much of earth and water wrought,   †
I must attend time's leisure with my moan;
   Receiving nought by elements so slow
   But heavy tears, badges of either's woe.

[XLIV]

18

37

The other two, slight air and purging fire,
Are both with thee, wherever I abide,
The first my thought, the other my desire,
These present-absent with swift motion slide
For when these quicker elements are gone
In tender embassy of love to thee,
My life, being made of four, with two alone
Sinks down to death, oppress'd with melancholy;
Until life's composition be recured
By those swift messengers return'd from thee,
Who even but now come back again, assured
Of thy fair health, recounting it to me:
  This told, I joy; but then no longer glad,
  I send them back again and straight grow sad.

[XLV]

38

Weary with toil, I haste me to my bed,
The dear repose for limbs with travel tired,
But then begins a journey in my head
To work my mind, when body's work's expired:
For then my thoughts, from far where I abide,
Intend a zealous pilgrimage to thee,
And keep my drooping eyelids open wide,
Looking on darkness which the blind do see:
Save that my soul's imaginary sight
Presents thy shadow to my sightless view,
Which, like a jewel, hung in ghastly night,   †
Makes black night beauteous, and her old face new.
  Lo, thus, by day my limbs, by night my mind,
  For thee, and for myself, no quiet find.

[XXVII]

19

39

When most I wink, then do mine eyes best see,
For all the day they view things unrespected,
But when I sleep, in dreams they look on thee,
And, darkly bright, are bright in dark directed.
Then thou, whose shadow shadows doth make bright,
How would thy shadow's form form happy show
To the clear day with thy much clearer light,
When to unseeing eyes thy shade shines so?
How would, I say, mine eyes be blessed made
By looking on thee in the living day,
When in dead night thy fair imperfect shade
Through heavy sleep on sightless eyes doth stay?
   All days are nights to see till I see thee,
   And nights bright days when dreams do show thee me.

[XLIII]

40

Is it thy will thy image should keep open
My heavy eyelids to the weary night?
Dost thou desire my slumbers should be broken,
While shadows like to thee do mock my sight?
Is it thy spirit that thou send'st from thee
So far from home into my deeds to pry,
To find out shames and idle hours in me,
The scope and tenure of thy jealousy?
O, no! thy love, though much, is not so great,
It is my love that keeps mine eye awake,
Mine own true love that doth my rest defeat,
To play the watchman ever for thy sake:
   For thee watch I, whilst thou doth wake elsewhere,
   From me far off, with others all too near.

[LXI]

41

How can I then return in happy plight,
That am debarr'd the benefit of rest?
When day's oppression is not eas'd by night,
But day by night and night by day oppress'd?
And each (though enemies to either's reign)
Do in consent shake hands to torture me,
The one by toil, the other to complain
How far I toil, still farther off from thee.
I tell the day to please him thou art bright,   †
And dost him grace when clouds do blot the heaven:
So flatter I the swart-complexion'd night,
When sparkling stars twire not thou gild'st the even.
   But day doth daily draw my sorrows longer,
   And night doth nightly make grief's strength seem   †
     stronger.

[XXVIII]

42

That time of year thou mayst in me behold
When yellow leaves, or none, or few, do hang
Upon those boughs which shake against the cold,
Bare ruin'd choirs, where late the sweet birds sang.
In me thou see'st the twilight of such day
As after sunset fadeth in the west,
Which by and by black night doth take away,
Death's second self that seals up all in rest.
In me thou see'st the glowing of such fire,
That on the ashes of his youth doth lie,
As the death-bed, whereon it must expire
Consum'd with that which it was nourish'd by.
   This thou perceiv'st, which makes thy love more strong,
   To love that well, which thou must leave ere long.

[LXXIII]

43

But be contented, when that fell arrest †
Without all bail shall carry me away,
My life hath in this line some interest,
Which for memorial still with thee shall stay.
When thou reviewest this, thou dost review
The very part was consecrate to thee;
The earth can have but earth, which is his due,
My spirit is thine, the better part of me:
So then thou hast but lost the dregs of life,
The prey of worms, my body being dead,
The coward conquest of a wretch's knife, †
Too base of thee to be remembered.
   The worth of that is that which it contains,
   And that is this, and this with thee remains.

[LXXIV]

44

Or I shall live your epitaph to make,
Or you survive when I in earth am rotten;
From hence your memory death cannot take,
Although in me each part will be forgotten.
Your name from hence immortal life shall have,
Though I, once gone, to all the world must die:
The earth can yield me but a common grave,
When you entombed in men's eyes shall lie.
Your monument shall be my gentle verse,
Which eyes not yet created shall o'er-read,
And tongues to be your being shall rehearse,
When all the breathers of this world are dead;
   You still shall live (such virtue hath my pen)
   Where breath most breathes, even in the mouths of
     men.

[LXXXI]

45

Tir'd with all these, for restful death I cry,
As, to behold desert a beggar born,
And needy nothing trimm'd in jollity,
And purest faith unhappily forsworn,
And gilded honour shamefully misplac'd,
And maiden virtue rudely strumpeted,
And right perfection wrongfully disgrac'd,
And strength by limping sway disabled,
And art made tongue-tied by authority,
And folly, doctor-like, controlling skill,
And simple truth miscall'd simplicity,
And captive good attending captain ill:
   Tir'd with all these, from these would I be gone,
   Save that, to die, I leave my love alone.

[LXVI]

46

No longer mourn for me when I am dead
Than you shall hear the surly sullen bell
Give warning to the world that I am fled
From this vile world with vilest worms to dwell:
Nay, if you read this line, remember not
The hand that writ it, for I love you so,
That I in your sweet thoughts would be forgot,
If thinking on me then should make you woe.   †
O if, I say, you look upon this verse,
When I perhaps compounded am with clay,   †
Do not so much as my poor name rehearse,
But let your love even with my life decay;
   Lest the wise world should look into your moan,
   And mock you with me after I am gone.

[LXXI]

23

47

If thou survive my well-contented day,
When that churl Death my bones with dust shall cover,
And shalt by fortune once more re-survey
These poor rude lines of thy deceased lover,
Compare them with the bettering of the time,
And though they be outstripp'd by every pen,
Reserve them for my love, not for their rhyme,
Exceeded by the height of happier men.
Oh then vouchsafe me but this loving thought:
'Had my friend's Muse grown with this growing age,
A dearer birth than this his love had brought,
To march in ranks of better equipage:
    But since he died, and poets better prove,
    Theirs for their style I'll read, his for his love.'

[xxxii]

48

O, lest the world should task you to recite
What merit liv'd in me that you should love,
After my death, dear love, forget me quite,
For you in me can nothing worthy prove;
Unless you would devise some virtuous lie,
To do more for me than mine own desert,
And hang more praise upon deceased I
Than niggard truth would willingly impart:
O, lest your true love may seem false in this,
That you for love speak well of me untrue,
My name be buried where my body is,
And live no more to shame nor me, nor you.
    For I am sham'd by that which I bring forth,
    And so should you, to love things nothing worth.

[lxxii]

49

Alack, what poverty my Muse brings forth,
That having such a scope to show her pride,
The argument all bare is of more worth
Than when it hath my added praise beside!
Oh blame me not, if I no more can write!
Look in your glass, and there appears a face
That over-goes my blunt invention quite,
Dulling my lines, and doing me disgrace.
Were it not sinful then, striving to mend,   †
To mar the subject that before was well?
For to no other pass my verses tend
Than of your graces and your gifts to tell;
   And more, much more than in my verse can sit,
   Your own glass shows you, when you look in it.

                                 [CIII]

50

Who is it that says most, which can say more
Than this rich praise, that you alone are you,
In whose confine immured is the store
Which should example where your equal grew?
Lean penury within that pen doth dwell
That to his subject lends not some small glory,
But he that writes of you, if he can tell
That you are you, so dignifies his story.
Let him but copy what in you is writ,
Not making worse what nature made so clear,
And such a counterpart shall fame his wit,
Making his style admired every where.
   You to your beauteous blessings add a curse,
   Being fond on praise, which makes your praises   †
   worse.

                                 [LXXXIV]

51

My tongue-tied Muse in manners holds her still,
While comments of your praise, richly compil'd,
Reserve their character with golden quill,   †
And precious phrase by all the Muses fil'd.
I think good thoughts, whilst other write good words,
And like unletter'd clerk still cry 'Amen'
To every hymn that able spirit affords,
In polish'd form of well refined pen.
Hearing you prais'd, I say ''Tis so, 'tis true,'
And to the most of praise add something more,
But that is in my thought, whose love to you,
Though words come hindmost, holds his rank before.
   Then others for the breath of words respect,
   Me for my dumb thoughts, speaking in effect.

[LXXXV]

52

Was it the proud full sail of his great verse,
Bound for the prize of (all too precious) you,
That did my ripe thoughts in my brain inhearse,
Making their tomb the womb wherein they grew?   †
Was it his spirit, by spirits taught to write
Above a mortal pitch, that struck me dead?
No, neither he, nor his compeers by night
Giving him aid, my verse astonished.
He, nor that affable familiar ghost
Which nightly gulls him with intelligence,
As victors of my silence cannot boast,
I was not sick of any fear from thence:
   But when your countenance fill'd up his line,
   Then lack'd I matter, that enfeebled mine.

[LXXXVI]

53

O, how I faint when I of you do write,
Knowing a better spirit doth use your name,
And in the praise thereof spends all his might,
To make me tongue-tied speaking of your fame!
But since your worth, wide as the ocean is,
The humble as the proudest sail doth bear,
My saucy bark, inferior far to his,
On your broad main doth wilfully appear.
Your shallowest help will hold me up afloat,
Whilst he upon your soundless deep doth ride,
Or, being wreck'd, I am a worthless boat,
He of tall building, and of goodly pride:
   Then if he thrive and I be cast away,
   The worst was this, my love was my decay.

[LXXX]

54

Whilst I alone did call upon thy aid,
My verse alone had all thy gentle grace,
But now my gracious numbers are decay'd,
And my sick Muse doth give another place.
I grant, sweet love, thy lovely argument
Deserves the travail of a worthier pen,
Yet what of thee thy poet doth invent
He robs thee of, and pays it thee again;
He lends thee virtue, and he stole that word
From thy behaviour; beauty doth he give,
And found it in thy cheek: he can afford
No praise to thee but what in thee doth live.
   Then thank him not for that which he doth say,
   Since what he owes thee thou thyself dost pay.

[LXXIX]

55

O truant Muse, what shall be thy amends
For thy neglect of truth in beauty dyed?
Both truth and beauty on my love depends;
So dost thou too, and therein dignified.
Make answer, Muse; wilt thou not haply say,
'Truth needs no colour, with his colour fix'd;
Beauty no pencil, beauty's truth to lay;
But best is best, if never intermix'd'?
Because he needs no praise, wilt thou be dumb?
Excuse not silence so, for 't lies in thee
To make him much outlive a gilded tomb,
And to be prais'd of ages yet to be.
    Then do thy office, Muse, I teach thee how,
    To make him seem long hence as he shows now.

[CI]

56

I never saw that you did painting need,
And therefore to your fair no painting set;
I found (or thought I found) you did exceed
The barren tender of a poet's debt:
And therefore have I slept in your report,
That you yourself, being extant, well might show
How far a modern quill doth come too short,
Speaking of worth, what worth in you doth grow.
This silence for my sin you did impute,
Which shall be most my glory, being dumb;
For I impair not beauty being mute,
When others would give life, and bring a tomb:
    There lives more life in one of your fair eyes,
    Than both your poets can in praise devise.

[LXXXIII]

57

Let not my love be call'd idolatry,
Nor my beloved as an idol show,
Since all alike my songs and praises be
To one, of one, still such, and ever so.
Kind is my love to-day, to-morrow kind,
Still constant in a wondrous excellence;
Therefore my verse to constancy confin'd,
One thing expressing, leaves out difference.
'Fair, kind, and true,' is all my argument,
'Fair, kind, and true,' varying to other words;
And in this change is my invention spent,
Three themes in one, which wondrous scope affords.
　　'Fair, kind, and true,' have often liv'd alone,
　　Which three, till now, never kept seat in one.

　　　　　　　　　　　　　　　　　　[cv]

58

How can my Muse want subject to invent,
While thou dost breathe, that pour'st into my verse
Thine own sweet argument, too excellent
For every vulgar paper to rehearse?
Oh give thyself the thanks, if aught in me
Worthy perusal stand against thy sight,
For who's so dumb that cannot write to thee,
When thou thyself dost give invention light?
Be thou the tenth Muse, ten times more in worth
Than those old nine which rhymers invocate,
And he that calls on thee, let him bring forth
Eternal numbers to outlive long date.
　　If my slight Muse do please these curious days,
　　The pain be mine, but thine shall be the praise.

　　　　　　　　　　　　　　　　　[xxxviii]

59

So oft have I invok'd thee for my Muse,
And found such fair assistance in my verse,
As every alien pen hath got my use
And under thee their poesy disperse.
Thine eyes, that taught the dumb on high to sing,
And heavy ignorance aloft to fly,   †
Have added feathers to the learned's wing,
And given grace a double majesty.
Yet be most proud of that which I compile,
Whose influence is thine, and born of thee:
In others' works thou dost but mend the style,
And arts with thy sweet graces graced be:
   But thou art all my art, and dost advance
   As high as learning my rude ignorance.

[LXXVIII]

60

I grant thou wert not married to my Muse,
And therefore mayst without attaint o'erlook
The dedicated words which writers use
Of their fair subject, blessing every book.
Thou art as fair in knowledge as in hue,
Finding thy worth a limit past my praise,
And therefore art enforc'd to seek anew
Some fresher stamp of the time-bettering days;
And do so, love, yet when they have devis'd
What strained touches rhetoric can lend,
Thou, truly fair, wert truly sympathiz'd,
In true plain words, by thy true-telling friend;
   And their gross painting might be better us'd   †
   Where cheeks need blood; in thee it is abus'd.

[LXXXII]

61

So is it not with me as with that Muse,
Stirr'd by a painted beauty to his verse,
Who heaven itself for ornament doth use
And every fair with his fair doth rehearse,
Making a couplement of proud compare
With sun and moon, with earth and sea's rich gems,
With April's first-born flowers, and all things rare,
That heaven's air in this huge rondure hems;
O let me, true in love, but truly write,
And then believe me, my love is as fair
As any mother's child, though not so bright
As those gold candles fix'd in heaven's air:
   Let them say more that like of hearsay well,
   I will not praise that purpose not to sell.   †

[XXI]

62

That thou art blam'd shall not be thy defect,
For slander's mark was ever yet the fair;
The ornament of beauty is suspect,
A crow that flies in heaven's sweetest air.
So thou be good, slander doth but approve
Thy worth the greater, being woo'd of time;   †
For canker vice the sweetest buds doth love,
And thou present'st a pure unstained prime.
Thou hast pass'd by the ambush of young days,
Either not assail'd, or victor being charg'd,
Yet this thy praise cannot be so thy praise,
To tie up envy evermore enlarg'd:
   If some suspect of ill mask'd not thy show,
   Then thou alone kingdoms of hearts shouldst owe.

[LXX]

31

63

Those parts of thee that the world's eye doth view
Want nothing that the thought of hearts can mend;
All tongues (the voice of souls) give thee that due,
Uttering bare truth, even so as foes commend.
Thy outward thus with outward praise is crown'd,
But those same tongues, that give thee so thine own,
In other accents do this praise confound
By seeing farther than the eye hath shown.
They look into the beauty of thy mind,
And that in guess they measure by thy deeds;
Then, churls, their thoughts, although their eyes were
    kind,
To thy fair flower add the rank smell of weeds:
  But why thy odour matcheth not thy show,
    The soil is this, that thou dost common grow.   †

[LXIX]

64

Ah, wherefore with infection should he live,
And with his presence grace impiety,
That sin by him advantage should achieve,
And lace itself with his society?
Why should false painting imitate his cheek,
And steal dead seeing of his living hue?   †
Why should poor beauty indirectly seek
Roses of shadow, since his rose is true?
Why should he live, now Nature bankrupt is,
Beggar'd of blood to blush through lively veins?
For she hath no exchequer now but his,
And, proud of many, lives upon his gains.   †
  O, him she stores, to show what wealth she had
    In days long since, before these last so bad.

[LXVII]

65

O, how much more doth beauty beauteous seem
By that sweet ornament which truth doth give!
The rose looks fair, but fairer we it deem
For that sweet odour, which doth in it live.
The canker-blooms have full as deep a dye
As the perfumed tincture of the roses,
Hang on such thorns, and play as wantonly,
When summer's breath their masked buds discloses: †
But, for their virtue only is their show,
They live unwoo'd, and unrespected fade;
Die to themselves. Sweet roses do not so,
Of their sweet deaths are sweetest odours made:
   And so of you, beauteous and lovely youth,
   When that shall vade, by verse distills your truth.

[LIV]

66

Full many a glorious morning have I seen
Flatter the mountain-tops with sovereign eye,
Kissing with golden face the meadows green,
Gilding pale streams with heavenly alchemy;
Anon permit the basest clouds to ride
With ugly rack on his celestial face,
And from the forlorn world his visage hide,
Stealing unseen to rest with this disgrace: †
Even so my sun one early morn did shine
With all-triumphant splendour on my brow;
But, out, alack! he was but one hour mine,
The region cloud hath mask'd him from me now.   †
   Yet him for this my love no whit disdaineth;
   Suns of the world may stain when heaven's sun
     staineth.

[XXXIII]

67

Why didst thou promise such a beauteous day,
And make me travel forth without my cloak,
To let base clouds o'ertake me in my way,
Hiding thy bravery in their rotten smoke?
'Tis not enough that through the cloud thou break,
To dry the rain on my storm-beaten face,
For no man well of such a salve can speak,
That heals the wound, and cures not the disgrace:
Nor can thy shame give physic to my grief,
Though thou repent, yet I have still the loss;
The offender's sorrow lends but weak relief
To him that bears the strong offence's cross.   †
   Ah, but those tears are pearl which thy love sheds,
   And they are rich, and ransom all ill deeds.

[xxxiv]

68

That thou hast her, it is not all my grief,
And yet it may be said I lov'd her dearly;
That she hath thee, is of my wailing chief,
A loss in love that touches me more nearly.
Loving offenders, thus I will excuse ye;
Thou dost love her, because thou know'st I love her,
And for my sake even so doth she abuse me,
Suffering my friend for my sake to approve her.
If I lose thee, my loss is my love's gain,
And losing her, my friend hath found that loss;
Both find each other, and I lose both twain,
And both for my sake lay on me this cross:
   But here's the joy; my friend and I are one;
   Sweet flattery! then she loves but me alone.

[xlii]

69

Take all my loves, my love, yea, take them all;
What hast thou then more than thou hadst before?
No love, my love, that thou mayst true love call,
All mine was thine, before thou hadst this more.
Then if for my love thou my love receivest,
I cannot blame thee, for my love thou usest,
But yet be blam'd, if thou thyself deceivest
By wilful taste of what thyself refusest.
I do forgive thy robbery, gentle thief,
Although thou steal thee all my poverty:
And yet love knows it is a greater grief
To bear love's wrong than hate's known injury.
  Lascivious grace, in whom all ill well shows,
  Kill me with spites; yet we must not be foes.

[XL]

70

How sweet and lovely dost thou make the shame
Which, like a canker in the fragrant rose,
Doth spot the beauty of thy budding name!
Oh, in what sweets dost thou thy sins inclose!
That tongue that tells the story of thy days,
(Making lascivious comments on thy sport)
Cannot dispraise, but in a kind of praise,   †
Naming thy name, blesses an ill report.
Oh what a mansion have those vices got
Which for their habitation chose out thee,
Where beauty's veil doth cover every blot,
And all things turn to fair that eyes can see!
  Take heed, dear heart, of this large privilege;
  The hardest knife ill us'd doth lose his edge.

[XCV]

35

71

Some say thy fault is youth, some wantonness,
Some say thy grace is youth and gentle sport;
Both grace and faults are lov'd of more and less:
Thou mak'st faults graces that to thee resort.
As on the finger of a throned queen
The basest jewel will be well esteem'd,
So are those errors, that in thee are seen,
To truths translated, and for true things deem'd.
How many lambs might the stern wolf betray,
If like a lamb he could his looks translate!
How many gazers mightst thou lead away,
If thou wouldst use the strength of all thy state!
　　But do not so; I love thee in such sort,
　　As thou being mine, mine is thy good report.

[xcvi]

72

But do thy worst to steal thyself away,
For term of life thou art assured mine:
And life no longer than thy love will stay,
For it depends upon that love of thine.
Then need I not to fear the worst of wrongs,
When in the least of them my life hath end.
I see a better state to me belongs
Than that which on thy humour doth depend:
Thou canst not vex me with inconstant mind,
Since that my life on thy revolt doth lie;
Oh what a happy title do I find,
Happy to have thy love, happy to die!
　　But what's so blessed-fair that fears no blot?
　　Thou mayst be false, and yet I know it not.

[xcii]

SONNETS

73

Being your slave, what should I do but tend
Upon the hours and times of your desire?
I have no precious time at all to spend,
Nor services to do, till you require.
Nor dare I chide the world-without-end hour,   †
Whilst I (my sovereign) watch the clock for you,
Nor think the bitterness of absence sour,
When you have bid your servant once adieu;
Nor dare I question with my jealous thought
Where you may be, or your affairs suppose,
But like a sad slave stay and think of nought
Save where you are, how happy you make those.
   So true a fool is love, that in your Will,
   Though you do any thing, he thinks no ill.

[LVII]

74

So shall I live, supposing thou art true,
Like a deceived husband; so love's face
May still seem love to me, though alter'd new;
Thy looks with me, thy heart in other place:
For there can live no hatred in thine eye,
Therefore in that I cannot know thy change.
In many's looks the false heart's history
Is writ in moods and frowns and wrinkles strange;
But heaven in thy creation did decree
That in thy face sweet love should ever dwell,
Whate'er thy thoughts, or thy heart's workings be,
Thy looks should nothing thence but sweetness tell.
   How like Eve's apple doth thy beauty grow,
   If thy sweet virtue answer not thy show!

[XCIII]

75

That god forbid, that made me first your slave,
I should in thought control your times of pleasure,
Or at your hand the account of hours to crave,
Being your vassal bound to stay your leisure!
O, let me suffer (being at your beck)
The imprison'd absence of your liberty, †
And patience, tame to sufferance, bide each check,
Without accusing you of injury.
Be where you list, your charter is so strong,
That you yourself may privilege your time
To what you will; to you it doth belong †
Yourself to pardon of self-doing crime.
    I am to wait, though waiting so be hell,
    Not blame your pleasure, be it ill or well.

[LVIII]

76

When thou shalt be dispos'd to set me light,
And place my merit in the eye of scorn,
Upon thy side against myself I'll fight,
And prove thee virtuous, though thou art forsworn.
With mine own weakness being best acquainted,
Upon thy part I can set down a story
Of faults conceal'd, wherein I am attainted,
That thou in losing me shall win much glory:
And I by this will be a gainer too;
For bending all my loving thoughts on thee,
The injuries that to myself I do,
Doing thee vantage, double-vantage me.
    Such is my love, to thee I so belong,
    That for thy right myself will bear all wrong.

[LXXXVIII]

77

Say that thou didst forsake me for some fault,
And I will comment upon that offence:
Speak of my lameness, and I straight will halt,
Against thy reasons making no defence.
Thou canst not, love, disgrace me half so ill,
To set a form upon desired change,
As I'll myself disgrace; knowing thy will,
I will acquaintance strangle and look strange;
Be absent from thy walks; and in my tongue
Thy sweet beloved name no more shall dwell,
Lest I, too much profane, should do it wrong,
And haply of our old acquaintance tell.
    For thee, against myself I'll vow debate,
    For I must ne'er love him whom thou dost hate.

[LXXXIX]

78

No more be griev'd at that which thou hast done;
Roses have thorns, and silver fountains mud,
Clouds and eclipses stain both moon and sun,
And loathsome canker lives in sweetest bud.
All men make faults, and even I in this,
Authorizing thy trespass with compare,
Myself corrupting salving thy amiss,
Excusing thy sins more than thy sins are;
For to thy sensual fault I bring in sense—
Thy adverse party is thy advocate—
And 'gainst myself a lawful plea commence;
Such civil war is in my love and hate,
    That I an accessary needs must be
    To that sweet thief which sourly robs from me.

[XXXV]

79

Those pretty wrongs that liberty commits,
When I am sometime absent from thy heart,
Thy beauty and thy years full well befits,
For still temptation follows where thou art.
Gentle thou art, and therefore to be won,   †
Beauteous thou art, therefore to be assailed;
And when a woman woos, what woman's son
Will sourly leave her till he have prevailed?   ˙†
Ay me! but yet thou mightst my seat forbear,   †
And chide thy beauty, and thy straying youth,
Who lead thee in their riot even there
Where thou art forc'd to break a twofold truth;
   Hers by thy beauty tempting her to thee,
   Thine by thy beauty being false to me.

[XLI]

80

How like a winter hath my absence been
From thee, the pleasure of the fleeting year!
What freezings have I felt, what dark days seen!
What old December's bareness every where!
And yet this time remov'd was summer's time;
The teeming autumn, big with rich increase,
Bearing the wanton burthen of the prime,
Like widowed wombs after their lords' decease:
Yet this abundant issue seem'd to me
But hope of orphans, and unfather'd fruit;
For summer and his pleasures wait on thee,
And, thou away, the very birds are mute;
   Or, if they sing, 'tis with so dull a cheer
   That leaves look pale, dreading the winter's near.

[XCVII]

81

Sweet love, renew thy force; be it not said
Thy edge should blunter be than appetite,
Which but to-day by feeding is allay'd,
To-morrow sharpen'd in his former might:
So, love, be thou; although to-day thou fill
Thy hungry eyes, even till they wink with fulness,
To-morrow see again, and do not kill
The spirit of love with a perpetual dulness.
Let this sad interim like the ocean be
Which parts the shore, where two contracted new
Come daily to the banks, that, when they see
Return of love, more blest may be the view;
 Or call it winter, which, being full of care,   †
 Makes summer's welcome, thrice more wish'd, more
  rare.

              [LVI]

82

From you have I been absent in the spring,
When proud-pied April, dress'd in all his trim,
Hath put a spirit of youth in every thing:
That heavy Saturn laugh'd and leap'd with him.
Yet nor the lays of birds, nor the sweet smell
Of different flowers in odour and in hue,
Could make me any summer's story tell:
Or from their proud lap pluck them where they grew:
Nor did I wonder at the lily's white,
Nor praise the deep vermilion in the rose,
They were but sweet, but figures of delight:
Drawn after you, you pattern of all those.
 Yet seem'd it winter still, and, you away,
 As with your shadow I with these did play.

             [XCVIII]

83

My love is strengthen'd, though more weak in seeming,
I love not less, though less the show appear:
That love is merchandiz'd, whose rich esteeming   †
The owner's tongue doth publish every where.
Our love was new, and then but in the spring,
When I was wont to greet it with my lays,
As Philomel in summer's front doth sing,
And stops his pipe in growth of riper days:
Not that the summer is less pleasant now
Than when her mournful hymns did hush the night,
But that wild music burthens every bough,
And sweets grown common lose their dear delight.
  Therefore, like her, I sometime hold my tongue,
  Because I would not dull you with my song.

[cii]

84

Where art thou, Muse, that thou forget'st so long
To speak of that which gives thee all thy might?
Spend'st thou thy fury on some worthless song,
Darkening thy power to lend base subjects light?
Return, forgetful Muse, and straight redeem
In gentle numbers time so idly spent,
Sing to the ear that doth thy lays esteem,
And gives thy pen both skill and argument.
Rise, resty Muse, my love's sweet face survey,
If Time have any wrinkle graven there,
If any, be a satire to decay,
And make Time's spoils despised every where.
  Give my love fame faster than Time wastes life,
  So thou prevent'st his scythe, and crooked knife.

[c]

85

Against my love shall be as I am now,
With Time's injurious hand crush'd and o'erworn,
When hours have drain'd his blood and fill'd his brow
With lines and wrinkles, when his youthful morn
Hath travell'd on to age's steepy night,
And all those beauties whereof now he's king
Are vanishing, or vanish'd out of sight,
Stealing away the treasure of his spring;
For such a time do I now fortify
Against confounding age's cruel knife,
That he shall never cut from memory
My sweet love's beauty, though my lover's life:
   His beauty shall in these black lines be seen,
   And they shall live, and he in them still green.

[LXIII]

86

Devouring Time, blunt thou the lion's paws,   †
And make the earth devour her own sweet brood,
Pluck the keen teeth from the fierce tiger's jaws,
And burn the long-lived phœnix in her blood,
Make glad and sorry seasons as thou fleets,
And do whate'er thou wilt, swift-footed Time,
To the wide world and all her fading sweets;
But I forbid thee one most heinous crime,
O, carve not with thy hours my love's fair brow,
Nor draw no lines there with thine antique pen,
Him in thy course untainted do allow,
For beauty's pattern to succeeding men.
   Yet do thy worst, old Time; despite thy wrong,
   My love shall in my verse ever live young.

[XIX]

87

Thus is his cheek the map of days outworn,
When beauty liv'd and died as flowers do now,
Before these bastard signs of fair were born,
Or durst inhabit on a living brow;
Before the golden tresses of the dead,   †
The right of sepulchres, were shorn away,
To live a second life on second head,
Ere beauty's dead fleece made another gay:
In him those holy antique hours are seen,
Without all ornament, itself and true,
Making no summer of another's green,
Robbing no old to dress his beauty new;
   And him as for a map doth Nature store,
   To show false Art what beauty was of yore.

[LXVIII]

88

To me, fair friend, you never can be old,
For as you were when first your eye I ey'd,
Such seems your beauty still. Three winters cold
Have from the forests shook three summers' pride,   †
Three beauteous springs to yellow autumn turn'd
In process of the seasons have I seen,
Three April perfumes in three hot Junes burn'd,
Since first I saw you fresh, which yet are green.
Ah, yet doth beauty, like a dial-hand,
Steal from his figure, and no pace perceiv'd,   †
So your sweet hue, which methinks still doth stand,
Hath motion, and mine eye may be deceiv'd:
   For fear of which, hear this, thou age unbred;
   Ere you were born was beauty's summer dead.

[CIV]

89

The forward violet thus did I chide,   †
'Sweet thief, whence didst thou steal thy sweet that
     smells,
If not from my love's breath? The purple pride
Which on thy soft cheek for complexion dwells
In my love's veins thou hast too grossly dyed.'
The lily I condemned for thy hand,
And buds of marjoram had stol'n thy hair;
The roses fearfully on thorns did stand,
One blushing shame, another white despair;
A third, nor red nor white, had stol'n of both,
And to his robbery had annex'd thy breath,
But, for his theft, in pride of all his growth
A vengeful canker eat him up to death.
    More flowers I noted, yet I none could see
    But sweet, or colour, it had stol'n from thee.

[xcix]

90

Thy glass will show thee how thy beauties wear,
Thy dial how thy precious minutes waste,
The vacant leaves thy mind's imprint will bear,   †
And of this book this learning mayst thou taste.
The wrinkles which thy glass will truly show
Of mouthed graves will give thee memory;
Thou by thy dial's shady stealth mayst know
Time's thievish progress to eternity.
Look, what thy memory cannot contain
Commit to these waste blanks, and thou shalt find   †
Those children nurs'd, deliver'd from thy brain,
To take a new acquaintance of thy mind.
    These offices, so oft as thou wilt look,
    Shall profit thee and much enrich thy book.

[lxxvii]

91

Thy gift, thy tables, are within my brain
Full character'd with lasting memory,
Which shall above that idle rank remain
Beyond all date even to eternity:
Or at the least, so long as brain and heart
Have faculty by nature to subsist,
Till each to raz'd oblivion yield his part
Of thee, thy record never can be miss'd.
That poor retention could not so much hold,
Nor need I tallies thy dear love to score,
Therefore to give them from me was I bold,
To trust those tables that receive thee more:
    To keep an adjunct to remember thee
    Were to import forgetfulness in me.

[CXXII]

92

Were 't aught to me I bore the canopy,
With my extern the outward honouring,
Or laid great bases for eternity,
Which prove more short than waste or ruining?
Have I not seen dwellers on form and favour
Lose all, and more, by paying too much rent,
For compound sweet forgoing simple savour,
Pitiful thrivers, in their gazing spent?
No, let me be obsequious in thy heart,
And take thou my oblation, poor but free,
Which is not mix'd with seconds, knows no art,
But mutual render only me for thee.
    Hence, thou suborn'd informer! a true soul
    When most impeach'd stands least in thy control.

[CXXV]

93

Why is my verse so barren of new pride?
So far from variation or quick change?
Why with the time do I not glance aside
To new-found methods, and to compounds strange?
Why write I still all one, ever the same,
And keep invention in a noted weed,
That every word doth almost tell my name,
Showing their birth, and where they did proceed?
O, know, sweet love, I always write of you,
And you and love are still my argument;
So all my best is dressing old words new,
Spending again what is already spent:
    For as the sun is daily new and old,
    So is my love still telling what is told.

[LXXVI]

94

No, Time, thou shalt not boast that I do change;
Thy pyramids built up with newer might
To me are nothing novel, nothing strange,
They are but dressings of a former sight:
Our dates are brief, and therefore we admire
What thou dost foist upon us that is old,
And rather make them born to our desire
Than think that we before have heard them told:
Thy registers and thee I both defy,
Not wondering at the present, nor the past,
For thy records, and what we see doth lie,
Made more or less by thy continual haste.
    This I do vow and this shall ever be,
    I will be true despite thy scythe and thee.

[CXXIII]

95

Those lines that I before have writ do lie,
Even those that said I could not love you dearer.
Yet then my judgement knew no reason why
My most full flame should afterwards burn clearer.
But reckoning Time, whose million'd accidents
Creep in 'twixt vows, and change decrees of kings,
Tan sacred beauty, blunt the sharp'st intents,
Divert strong minds to the course of altering things;
Alas, why, fearing of Time's tyranny,
Might I not then say 'Now I love you best,'
When I was certain o'er incertainty,
Crowning the present, doubting of the rest?
   Love is a babe; then might I not say so,
    To give full growth to that which still doth grow?

[cxv]

96

If my dear love were but the child of state,
It might for Fortune's bastard be unfather'd,
As subject to Time's love, or to Time's hate,
Weeds among weeds, or flowers with flowers gather'd.
No, it was builded far from accident,
It suffers not in smiling pomp, nor falls
Under the blow of thralled discontent,
Whereto the inviting time our fashion calls:
It fears not policy, that heretic,
Which works on leases of short-number'd hours,
But all alone stands hugely politic,
That it nor grows with heat, nor drowns with showers:
   To this I witness call the fools of time,
    Which die for goodness, who have liv'd for crime.

[cxxiv]

97

Not mine own fears, nor the prophetic soul
Of the wide world, dreaming on things to come,
Can yet the lease of my true love control,
Suppos'd as forfeit to a confin'd doom.
The mortal moon hath her eclipse endur'd,   †
And the sad augurs mock their own presage;
Incertainties now crown themselves assur'd,
And peace proclaims olives of endless age.
Now with the drops of this most balmy time
My love looks fresh, and Death to me subscribes,
Since, spite of him, I'll live in this poor rhyme,
While he insults o'er dull and speechless tribes:
   And thou in this shalt find thy monument,
   When tyrants' crests and tombs of brass are spent.

[CVII]

98

Not marble, nor the gilded monuments
Of princes, shall outlive this powerful rhyme,
But you shall shine more bright in these contents
Than unswept stone, besmear'd with sluttish time.
When wasteful war shall statues overturn,
And broils root out the work of masonry,
Nor Mars his sword, nor war's quick fire, shall burn
The living record of your memory.
'Gainst death, and all oblivious enmity,
Shall you pace forth, your praise shall still find room,
Even in the eyes of all posterity
That wear this world out to the ending doom.
   So, till the judgement that yourself arise,
   You live in this, and dwell in lovers' eyes.

[LV]

99 †

When in the chronicle of wasted time
I see descriptions of the fairest wights,
And beauty making beautiful old rhyme,
In praise of ladies dead, and lovely knights,
Then in the blazon of sweet beauty's best,
Of hand, of foot, of lip, of eye, of brow,
I see their antique pen would have express'd
Even such a beauty as you master now.
So all their praises are but prophecies
Of this our time, all you prefiguring,
And, for they look'd but with divining eyes,
They had not still enough your worth to sing: †
   For we, which now behold these present days,
   Have eyes to wonder, but lack tongues to praise.

[CVI]

100

If there be nothing new, but that which is
Hath been before, how are our brains beguil'd,
Which, labouring for invention, bear amiss
The second burthen of a former child!
O, that record could with a backward look,
Even of five hundred courses of the sun,
Show me your image in some antique book,
Since mind at first in character was done.
That I might see what the old world could say
To this composed wonder of your frame;
Whe'er we are mended, or whe'er better they,
Or whether revolution be the same.
   O sure I am the wits of former days
   To subjects worse have given admiring praise.

[LIX]

101

What's in the brain, that ink may character,
Which hath not figur'd to thee my true spirit?
What's new to speak, what now to register,   †
That may express my love, or thy dear merit?
Nothing, sweet boy; but yet, like prayers divine,
I must each day say o'er the very same,
Counting no old thing old, thou mine, I thine,
Even as when first I hallow'd thy fair name.
So that eternal love in love's fresh case
Weighs not the dust and injury of age,
Nor gives to necessary wrinkles place,
But makes antiquity for aye his page,
    Finding the first conceit of love there bred,
    Where time and outward form would show it dead.

                     [CVIII]

102   †

Lord of my love, to whom in vassalage
Thy merit hath my duty strongly knit,
To thee I send this written ambassage,   **6702**
To witness duty, not to show my wit:
Duty so great, which wit so poor as mine
May make seem bare, in wanting words to show it,
But that I hope some good conceit of thine
In thy soul's thought, all naked, will bestow it;
Till whatsoever star that guides my moving,
Points on me graciously with fair aspect,
And puts apparel on my tatter'd loving,
To show me worthy of thy sweet respect:
    Then may I dare to boast how I do love thee,
    Till then, not show my head where thou mayst
      prove me.

                     [XXVI]

103

As an unperfect actor on the stage,
Who with his fear is put besides his part,
Or some fierce thing replete with too much rage,
Whose strength's abundance weakens his own heart;
So I, for fear of trust, forget to say
The perfect ceremony of love's right,   †
And in mine own love's strength seem to decay,
O'ercharged with burthen of mine own love's might.
O, let my books be then the eloquence   †
And dumb presagers of my speaking breast,
Who plead for love, and look for recompense,
More than that tongue that more hath more express'd.
 O learn to read what silent love hath writ:
 To hear with eyes belongs to love's fine wit.

            [xxiii]

104

Against that time (if ever that time come)
When I shall see thee frown on my defects,
When as thy love hath cast his utmost sum,
Call'd to that audit by advis'd respects;
Against that time when thou shalt strangely pass,
And scarcely greet me with that sun, thine eye,
When love, converted from the thing it was,
Shall reasons find of settled gravity;
Against that time do I ensconce me here
Within the knowledge of mine own desert,
And this my hand against myself uprear,
To guard the lawful reasons on thy part:
 To leave poor me thou hast the strength of laws,
 Since why to love I can allege no cause.

            [xlix]

105

Since I left you, mine eye is in my mind,
And that which governs me to go about
Doth part his function, and is partly blind,
Seems seeing, but effectually is out;
For it no form delivers to the heart
Of bird, of flower, or shape, which it doth latch:
Of his quick objects hath the mind no part,
Nor his own vision holds what it doth catch;
For if it see the rud'st or gentlest sight,
The most sweet favour or deformed'st creature,
The mountain, or the sea, the day, or night,
The crow, or dove, it shapes them to your feature:
   Incapable of more, replete with you,
   My most true mind thus maketh mine untrue.   †

[CXIII]

106

Or whether doth my mind, being crown'd with you,
Drink up the monarch's plague, this flattery?
Or whether shall I say mine eye saith true,
And that your love taught it this alchemy,   †
To make of monsters, and things indigest,
Such cherubins as your sweet self resemble,
Creating every bad a perfect best,
As fast as objects to his beams assemble?
O, 'tis the first; 'tis flattery in my seeing,
And my great mind most kingly drinks it up;
Mine eye well knows what with his gust is 'greeing,
And to his palate doth prepare the cup:
   If it be poison'd, 'tis the lesser sin
   That mine eye loves it and doth first begin.

[CXIV]

107

        †

'Tis better to be vile than vile esteemed,
When not to be receives reproach of being,
And the just pleasure lost, which is so deemed
Not by our feeling, but by others' seeing:
For why should others' false adulterate eyes
Give salutation to my sportive blood?
Or on my frailties why are frailer spies,
Which in their wills count bad what I think good?
No, I am that I am, and they that level
At my abuses reckon up their own;
I may be straight, though they themselves be bevel,
By their rank thoughts my deeds must not be shown;
   Unless this general evil they maintain,
   All men are bad and in their badness reign.

                    [CXXI]

108

O never say that I was false of heart,
Though absence seem'd my flame to qualify;
As easy might I from myself depart
As from my soul which in thy breast doth lie:
That is my home of love; if I have rang'd,
Like him that travels I return again,
Just to the time, not with the time exchang'd,
So that myself bring water for my stain.
Never believe, though in my nature reign'd
All frailties that besiege all kinds of blood,   †
That it could so preposterously be stain'd,
To leave for nothing all thy sum of good;
   For nothing this wide universe I call,
   Save thou, my rose; in it thou art my all.

                    [CIX]

109

Accuse me thus, that I have scanted all
Wherein I should your great deserts repay,
Forgot upon your dearest love to call,
Whereto all bonds do tie me day by day,
That I have frequent been with unknown minds,
And given to time your own dear-purchas'd right,
That I have hoisted sail to all the winds
Which should transport me farthest from your sight.
Book both my wilfulness and errors down,
And on just proof surmise accumulate,
Bring me within the level of your frown,
But shoot not at me in your waken'd hate;
   Since my appeal says I did strive to prove
   The constancy and virtue of your love.

[cxvii]

110

Let me not to the marriage of true minds
Admit impediments; love is not love   †
Which alters when it alteration finds,
Or bends with the remover to remove:
O, no! it is an ever-fixed mark,
That looks on tempests and is never shaken;
It is the star to every wandering bark,
Whose worth's unknown, although his height be taken. †
Love's not Time's fool, though rosy lips and cheeks †
Within his bending sickle's compass come;
Love alters not with his brief hours and weeks,
But bears it out even to the edge of doom.   †
   If this be error and upon me prov'd,
   I never writ, nor no man ever lov'd.

[cxvi]

111

That you were once unkind befriends me now,
And for that sorrow, which I then did feel,
Needs must I under my transgression bow,
Unless my nerves were brass or hammer'd steel.
For if you were by my unkindness shaken,
As I by yours, you've pass'd a hell of time,
And I, a tyrant, have no leisure taken
To weigh how once I suffer'd in your crime.
O, that our night of woe might have remember'd   †
My deepest sense, how hard true sorrow hits,
And soon to you, as you to me then tender'd
The humble salve, which wounded bosoms fits!
   But that your trespass now becomes a fee,
   Mine ransoms yours, and yours must ransom me.

[cxx]

112

Your love and pity doth the impression fill
Which vulgar scandal stamp'd upon my brow,
For what care I who calls me well or ill,
So you o'er-green my bad, my good allow?
You are my all the world, and I must strive
To know my shames and praises from your tongue;
None else to me, nor I to none alive,
That my steel'd sense or changes right or wrong.
In so profound abysm I throw all care
Of others' voices, that my adder's sense
To critic and to flatterer stopped are:
Mark how with my neglect I do dispense.
   You are so strongly in my purpose bred
   That all the world besides methinks are dead.   †

[cxii]

113

O, how thy worth with manners may I sing,
When thou art all the better part of me?
What can mine own praise to mine own self bring,
And what is 't but mine own when I praise thee?
Even for this let us divided live,
And our dear love lose name of single one,
That by this separation I may give
That due to thee which thou deserv'st alone.
O absence, what a torment wouldst thou prove,
Were it not thy sour leisure gave sweet leave
To entertain the time with thoughts of love,
Which time and thoughts so sweetly dost deceive,
   And that thou teachest how to make one twain,
   By praising him here who doth hence remain!

[XXXIX]

114

Let me confess that we two must be twain,
Although our undivided loves are one:
So shall those blots that do with me remain,
Without thy help, by me be borne alone.
In our two loves there is but one respect,
Though in our lives a separable spite,
Which though it alter not love's sole effect,
Yet doth it steal sweet hours from love's delight.
I may not evermore acknowledge thee,
Lest my bewailed guilt should do thee shame,
Nor thou with public kindness honour me,
Unless thou take that honour from thy name:
   But do not so; I love thee in such sort,
   As thou being mine, mine is thy good report.

[XXXVI]

115

Then hate me when thou wilt; if ever, now,
Now, while the world is bent my deeds to cross,
Join with the spite of fortune, make me bow,
And do not drop in for an after-loss:
Ah, do not, when my heart hath 'scaped this sorrow,
Come in the rearward of a conquer'd woe,
Give not a windy night a rainy morrow,
To linger out a purpos'd overthrow.
If thou wilt leave me, do not leave me last,
When other petty griefs have done their spite,
But in the onset come; so shall I taste
At first the very worst of fortune's might;
   And other strains of woe, which now seem woe,
   Compar'd with loss of thee will not seem so.

[xc]

116

When to the sessions of sweet silent thought
I summon up remembrance of things past,
I sigh the lack of many a thing I sought,
And with old woes new wail my dear time's waste:
Then can I drown an eye, unus'd to flow,
For precious friends hid in death's dateless night,
And weep afresh love's long since cancell'd woe,
And moan the expense of many a vanish'd sight:
Then can I grieve at grievances foregone,
And heavily from woe to woe tell o'er
The sad account of fore-bemoaned moan,
Which I new pay, as if not paid before.
   But if the while I think on thee, dear friend,
   All losses are restor'd, and sorrows end.

[xxx]

117

They that have power to hurt, and will do none,
That do not do the thing they most do show,
Who, moving others, are themselves as stone,
Unmoved, cold, and to temptation slow;
They rightly do inherit heaven's graces,
And husband nature's riches from expense,
They are the lords and owners of their faces,
Others but stewards of their excellence:
The summer's flower is to the summer sweet,
Though to itself it only live and die,
But if that flower with base infection meet,
The basest weed outbraves his dignity:
    For sweetest things turn sourest by their deeds,
    Lilies that fester smell far worse than weeds.   †

[xciv]

118

O, for my sake do you with Fortune chide,
The guilty goddess of my harmful deeds,
That did not better for my life provide
Than public means which public manners breeds.
Thence comes it that my name receives a brand,
And almost thence my nature is subdued
To what it works in, like the dyer's hand:
Pity me then, and wish I were renew'd;
Whilst, like a willing patient, I will drink
Potions of eisel 'gainst my strong infection;
No bitterness that I will bitter think,
Nor double penance to correct correction.
    Pity me then, dear friend, and I assure ye
    Even that your pity is enough to cure me.

[cxi]

119

Like as the waves make towards the pebbled shore,
So do our minutes hasten to their end,
Each changing place with that which goes before,
In sequent toil all forwards do contend.
Nativity, once in the main of light,
Crawls to maturity, wherewith being crown'd,
Crooked eclipses 'gainst his glory fight,
And Time that gave doth now his gift confound.
Time doth transfix the flourish set on youth,
And delves the parallels in beauty's brow,
Feeds on the rarities of nature's truth,
And nothing stands but for his scythe to mow.
   And yet to times in hope my verse shall stand,
   Praising thy worth, despite his cruel hand.

[LX]

120

When I have seen by Time's fell hand defaced
The rich proud cost of outworn buried age,
When sometime lofty towers I see down-razed,
And brass eternal slave to mortal rage;
When I have seen the hungry ocean gain
Advantage on the kingdom of the shore,
And the firm soil win of the watery main,
Increasing store with loss, and loss with store;
When I have seen such interchange of state,
Or state itself confounded to decay;
Ruin hath taught me thus to ruminate,
That Time will come and take my love away.
   This thought is as a death, which cannot choose
   But weep to have that which it fears to lose.

[LXIV]

121

As a decrepit father takes delight
To see his active child do deeds of youth,
So I, made lame by fortune's dearest spite,   †
Take all my comfort of thy worth and truth.
For whether beauty, birth, or wealth, or wit,
Or any of these all, or all, or more,
Intitled in thy parts, do crowned sit,
I make my love engrafted to this store:
So then I am not lame, poor, nor despis'd,
Whilst that this shadow doth such substance give
That I in thy abundance am suffic'd,
And by a part of all thy glory live:
  Look what is best, that best I wish in thee;
  This wish I have; then ten times happy me!

[xxxvii]

122

Alas 'tis true, I have gone here and there,
And made myself a motley to the view,
Gor'd mine own thoughts, sold cheap what is most dear,
Made old offences of affections new;
Most true it is that I have look'd on truth
Askance and strangely: but, by all above,
These blenches gave my heart another youth,
And worse essays prov'd thee my best of love.
Now all is done, have what shall have no end,
Mine appetite I never more will grind
On newer proof, to try an older friend,
A god in love, to whom I am confin'd.
  Then give me welcome, next my heaven the best,
  Even to thy pure and most most loving breast.

[cx]

123

What potions have I drunk of Siren tears,
Distill'd from limbecks foul as hell within,
Applying fears to hopes, and hopes to fears,
Still losing when I saw myself to win?
What wretched errors hath my heart committed,
Whilst it hath thought itself so blessed never?
How have mine eyes out of their spheres been fitted,   †
In the distraction of this madding fever?
O benefit of ill! now I find true
That better is by evil still made better;   †
And ruin'd love, when it is built anew,
Grows fairer than at first, more strong, far greater.
   So I return rebuk'd to my content,
   And gain by ills thrice more than I have spent.   †

[CXIX]

124

Like as to make our appetites more keen
With eager compounds we our palate urge,
As to prevent our maladies unseen
We sicken to shun sickness when we purge;
Even so, being full of your ne'er-cloying sweetness,
To bitter sauces did I frame my feeding;
And sick of welfare found a kind of meetness
To be diseas'd ere that there was true needing.
Thus policy in love, to anticipate
The ills that were not, grew to faults assured,
And brought to medicine a healthful state,
Which, rank of goodness, would by ill be cured:
   But thence I learn and find the lesson true,
   Drugs poison him that so fell sick of you.

[CXVIII]

125

When in disgrace with fortune and men's eyes,
I all alone beweep my outcast state,
And trouble deaf heaven with my bootless cries,
And look upon myself and curse my fate,
Wishing me like to one more rich in hope,
Featur'd like him, like him with friends possess'd,
Desiring this man's art, and that man's scope,
With what I most enjoy contented least;
Yet in these thoughts myself almost despising,
Haply I think on thee, and then my state,
(Like to the lark at break of day arising)
From sullen earth sings hymns at heaven's gate;   †
  For thy sweet love remember'd such wealth brings
  That then I scorn to change my state with kings.

[XXIX]

126

Farewell! thou art too dear for my possessing,
And like enough thou know'st thy estimate:
The charter of thy worth gives thee releasing,
My bonds in thee are all determinate.
For how do I hold thee but by thy granting?
And for that riches where is my deserving?
The cause of this fair gift in me is wanting,
And so my patent back again is swerving.
Thyself thou gav'st, thy own worth then not knowing,
Or me, to whom thou gav'st it, else mistaking;
So thy great gift, upon misprision growing,   †
Comes home again, on better judgement making.
  Thus have I had thee, as a dream doth flatter,   †
  In sleep a king, but waking no such matter.

[LXXXVII]

127

Those lips that Love's own hand did make
Breath'd forth the sound that said 'I hate,'
To me that languish'd for her sake:
But when she saw my woeful state,
Straight in her heart did mercy come,
Chiding that tongue that ever sweet
Was us'd in giving gentle doom;
And taught it thus anew to greet;
'I hate' she alter'd with an end,
That follow'd it as gentle day
Doth follow night, who, like a fiend,
From heaven to hell is flown away;
  'I hate' from hate away she threw,
  And sav'd my life, saying, 'not you.'

[CXLV]

128

How oft, when thou, my music, music play'st,
Upon that blessed wood whose motion sounds
With thy sweet fingers, when thou gently sway'st
The wiry concord that mine ear confounds,
Do I envy those jacks that nimble leap
To kiss the tender inward of thy hand,
Whilst my poor lips, which should that harvest reap,
At the wood's boldness by thee blushing stand:
To be so tickled, they would change their state
And situation with those dancing chips,
O'er whom thy fingers walk with gentle gait,
Making dead wood more blest than living lips:
  Since saucy jacks so happy are in this,
  Give them thy fingers, me thy lips to kiss.

[CXXVIII]

129

The little Love-god lying once asleep
Laid by his side his heart-inflaming brand,
Whilst many nymphs that vow'd chaste life to keep
Came tripping by; but in her maiden hand
The fairest votary took up that fire,
Which many legions of true hearts had warm'd;
And so the general of hot desire
Was sleeping by a virgin hand disarm'd.
This brand she quenched in a cool well by,
Which from Love's fire took heat perpetual,
Growing a bath and healthful remedy
For men diseas'd; but I, my mistress' thrall,
   Came there for cure, and this by that I prove,
   Love's fire heats water, water cools not love.

[CLIV]

130

Love is too young to know what conscience is,
Yet who knows not conscience is born of love?
Then, gentle cheater, urge not my amiss,
Lest guilty of my faults thy sweet self prove:
For, thou betraying me, I do betray
My nobler part to my gross body's treason;
My soul doth tell my body that he may
Triumph in love; flesh stays no farther reason,
But rising at thy name doth point out thee
As his triumphant prize; proud of this pride,
He is contented thy poor drudge to be,
To stand in thy affairs, fall by thy side.
   No want of conscience hold it that I call
   Her 'love' for whose dear love I rise and fall.

[CLI]

131

If thy soul check thee that I come so near,
Swear to thy blind soul that I was thy 'Will,'
And will, thy soul knows, is admitted there;
Thus far for love, my love-suit, sweet, fulfil.
'Will' will fulfil the treasure of thy love,
Ay, fill it full with wills, and my will one;
In things of great receipt with ease we prove
Among a number one is reckon'd none: †
Then in the number let me pass untold,
Though in thy store's account I one must be;
For nothing hold me, so it please thee hold
That nothing me, a something sweet to thee:
   Make but my name thy love, and love that still,
   And then thou lov'st me for my name is 'Will.'

[CXXXVI]

132

Whoever hath her wish, thou hast thy 'Will,'
And 'Will' to boot, and 'Will' in overplus;
More than enough am I that vex thee still,
To thy sweet will making addition thus.
Wilt thou, whose will is large and spacious,
Not once vouchsafe to hide my will in thine?
Shall will in others seem right gracious,
And in my will no fair acceptance shine?
The sea, all water, yet receives rain still,
And in abundance addeth to his store;
So thou, being rich in 'Will,' add to thy 'Will'
One will of mine, to make thy large 'Will' more.
   Let no unkind, no fair beseechers kill;   †
   Think all but one, and me in that one 'Will.'

[CXXXV]

133

Lo, as a careful housewife runs to catch
One of her feather'd creatures broke away,
Sets down her babe, and makes all swift dispatch
In pursuit of the thing she would have stay;
Whilst her neglected child holds her in chase,
Cries to catch her whose busy care is bent
To follow that which flies before her face,
Not prizing her poor infant's discontent;
So runn'st thou after that which flies from thee,
Whilst I thy babe chase thee afar behind;
But if thou catch thy hope, turn back to me,
And play the mother's part, kiss me, be kind:
  So will I pray that thou mayst have thy 'Will,'
  If thou turn back and my loud crying still.

[CXLIII]

134

So now I have confess'd that he is thine,
And I myself am mortgag'd to thy will,
Myself I'll forfeit, so that other mine
Thou wilt restore to be my comfort still:
But thou wilt not, nor he will not be free,
For thou art covetous, and he is kind;
He learn'd but suroty like to write for me,
Under that bond that him as fast doth bind.
The statute of thy beauty thou wilt take,
Thou usurer, that put'st forth all to use,
And sue a friend came debtor for my sake;
So him I lose through my unkind abuse.
  Him have I lost, thou hast both him and me,
  He pays the whole, and yet am I not free.

[CXXXIV]

135

Beshrew that heart that makes my heart to groan
For that deep wound it gives my friend and me!
Is 't not enough to torture me alone,
But slave to slavery my sweet'st friend must be?
Me from myself thy cruel eye hath taken,
And my next self thou harder hast engrossed;
Of him, myself, and thee, I am forsaken,
A torment thrice threefold thus to be crossed:
Prison my heart in thy steel bosom's ward,
But then my friend's heart let my poor heart bail;
Whoe'er keeps me, let my heart be his guard,
Thou canst not then use rigour in my gaol:
   And yet thou wilt; for I, being pent in thee,
   Perforce am thine, and all that is in me.

[CXXXIII]

136

In loving thee thou know'st I am forsworn,
But thou art twice forsworn, to me love swearing;
In act thy bed-vow broke, and new faith torn,
In vowing new hate after new love bearing.
But why of two oaths' breach do I accuse thee,
When I break twenty? I am perjur'd most,
For all my vows are oaths but to misuse thee,
And all my honest faith in thee is lost:
For I have sworn deep oaths of thy deep kindness,
Oaths of thy love, thy truth, thy constancy,
And, to enlighten thee, gave eyes to blindness,
Or made them swear against the thing they see;
   For I have sworn thee fair; more perjur'd I,   †
   To swear against the truth so foul a lie!

[CLII]

137

Love is my sin, and thy dear virtue hate,
Hate of my sin, grounded on sinful loving:
O but with mine compare thou thine own state,
And thou shalt find it merits not reproving,
Or, if it do, not from those lips of thine,
That have profan'd their scarlet ornaments,
And seal'd false bonds of love as oft as mine,
Robb'd others' beds' revenues of their rents.
Be it lawful I love thee as thou lov'st those
Whom thine eyes woo as mine importune thee,
Root pity in thy heart, that, when it grows,
Thy pity may deserve to pitied be.
  If thou dost seek to have what thou dost hide,
  By self-example mayst thou be denied!

[CXLII]

138

Be wise as thou art cruel, do not press
My tongue-tied patience with too much disdain;
Lest sorrow lend me words, and words express
The manner of my pity-wanting pain.
If I might teach thee wit, better it were,
Though not to love, yet, love, to tell me so,
As testy sick men, when their deaths be near,
No news but health from their physicians know;
For, if I should despair, I should grow mad,
And in my madness might speak ill of thee:
Now this ill-wresting world is grown so bad,
Mad slanderers by mad ears believed be.
  That I may not be so, nor thou belied,
  Bear thine eye straight, though thy proud heart go
    wide.

[CXL]

139

Thine eyes I love, and they, as pitying me,
Knowing thy heart torments me with disdain,
Have put on black, and loving mourners be,
Looking with pretty ruth upon my pain;
And truly not the morning sun of heaven
Better becomes the grey cheeks of the east,
Nor that full star that ushers in the even
Doth half that glory to the sober west,   †
As those two morning eyes become thy face: †
O, let it then as well beseem thy heart
To mourn for me, since mourning doth thee grace,
And suit thy pity like in every part.
   Then will I swear beauty herself is black,
   And all they foul that thy complexion lack.

[cxxxii]

140   †

In the old age black was not counted fair,
Or if it were, it bore not beauty's name;
But now is black beauty's successive heir,
And beauty slander'd with a bastard shame:
For since each hand hath put on nature's power,
Fairing the foul with art's false borrow'd face,
Sweet beauty hath no name, no holy bower,
But is profan'd, if not lives in disgrace.
Therefore my mistress' eyes are raven black,   †
Her eyes so suited, and they mourners seem
At such who, not born fair, no beauty lack,
Slandering creation with a false esteem:
   Yet so they mourn, becoming of their woe,
   That every tongue says beauty should look so.

[cxxvii]

141

Thou art as tyrannous, so as thou art,
As those whose beauties proudly make them cruel;
For well thou know'st to my dear doting heart
Thou art the fairest and most precious jewel.
Yet, in good faith, some say that thee behold,
Thy face hath not the power to make love groan;
To say they err I dare not be so bold,
Although I swear it to myself alone.
And to be sure that is not false I swear,
A thousand groans, but thinking on thy face,
One on another's neck, do witness bear
Thy black is fairest in my judgement's place.
   In nothing art thou black save in thy deeds,
   And thence this slander, as I think, proceeds.

[CXXXI]

142

In faith, I do not love thee with mine eyes,
For they in thee a thousand errors note,
But 'tis my heart that loves what they despise,
Who in despite of view is pleas'd to dote;
Nor are mine ears with thy tongue's tune delighted,
Nor tender feeling to base touches prone,
Nor taste, nor smell, desire to be invited
To any sensual feast with thee alone:
But my five wits nor my five senses can
Dissuade one foolish heart from serving thee,
Who leaves unsway'd the likeness of a man,
Thy proud heart's slave and vassal wretch to be:
   Only my plague thus far I count my gain,
   That she that makes me sin awards me pain.

[CXLI]

143

Thou blind fool, Love, what dost thou to mine eyes,
That they behold, and see not what they see?
They know what beauty is, see where it lies,
Yet what the best is take the worst to be.
If eyes, corrupt by over-partial looks,
Be anchor'd in the bay where all men ride,
Why of eyes' falsehood hast thou forged hooks,
Whereto the judgement of my heart is tied?
Why should my heart think that a several plot †
Which my heart knows the wide world's common place?
Or mine eyes seeing this, say this is not,
To put fair truth upon so foul a face?
   In things right true my heart and eyes have erred,
   And to this false plague are they now transferred.

[CXXXVII]

144 †

When my love swears that she is made of truth,
I do believe her though I know she lies,
That she might think me some untutor'd youth,
Unlearned in the world's false subtleties.
Thus vainly thinking that she thinks me young,
Although she knows my days are past the best,
Simply I credit her false-speaking tongue,
On both sides thus is simple truth suppress'd.
But wherefore says she not she is unjust?
And wherefore say not I that I am old?
O, love's best habit is in seeming trust,
And age in love loves not to have years told:
   Therefore I lie with her, and she with me,
   And in our faults by lies we flatter'd be.

[CXXXVIII]

145

O call not me to justify the wrong
That thy unkindness lays upon my heart;
Wound me not with thine eye, but with thy tongue;
Use power with power, and slay me not by art.
Tell me thou lov'st elsewhere, but in my sight,
Dear heart, forbear to glance thine eye aside;
What need'st thou wound with cunning, when thy might
Is more than my o'er-press'd defence can bide?
Let me excuse thee: ah, my love well knows
Her pretty looks have been mine enemies,
And therefore from my face she turns my foes,
That they elsewhere might dart their injuries:
    Yet do not so, but since I am near slain,
    Kill me outright with looks, and rid my pain.

[CXXXIX]

146

Canst thou, O cruel! say I love thee not,
When I against myself with thee partake?
Do I not think on thee, when I forgot
Am of myself, all tyrant for thy sake?
Who hateth thee that I do call my friend?
On whom frown'st thou that I do fawn upon?
Nay, if thou lour'st on me, do I not spend
Revenge upon myself with present moan?
What merit do I in myself respect,
That is so proud thy service to despise,
When all my best doth worship thy defect,
Commanded by the motion of thine eyes?
    But, love, hate on, for now I know thy mind;
    Those that can see thou lov'st, and I am blind.

[CXLIX]

147

Cupid laid by his brand and fell asleep:
A maid of Dian's this advantage found,
And his love-kindling fire did quickly steep
In a cold valley-fountain of that ground;
Which borrow'd from this holy fire of Love
A dateless lively heat, still to endure,
And grew a seething bath, which yet men prove
Against strange maladies a sovereign cure.
But at my mistress' eye Love's brand new-fired,
The boy for trial needs would touch my breast;
I, sick withal, the help of bath desired,
And thither hied, a sad distemper'd guest;
   But found no cure: the bath for my help lies
   Where Cupid got new fire, my mistress' eyes.

[CLIII]

148

My mistress' eyes are nothing like the sun,
Coral is far more red than her lips' red,
If snow be white, why then her breasts are dun,
If hairs be wires, black wires grow on her head:
I have seen roses damask'd, red and white,   †
But no such roses see I in her cheeks,
And in some perfumes is there more delight
Than in the breath that from my mistress reeks.
I love to hear her speak, yet well I know
That music hath a far more pleasing sound:
I grant I never saw a goddess go,
My mistress when she walks treads on the ground:
   And yet, by heaven, I think my love as rare
   As any she belied with false compare.

[CXXX]

149

O me, what eyes hath Love put in my head,
Which have no correspondence with true sight!
Or, if they have, where is my judgement fled,
That censures falsely what they see aright?
If that be fair whereon my false eyes dote,
What means the world to say it is not so?
If it be not, then love doth well denote
Love's eye is not so true as all men's: no,   †
How can it? O, how can Love's eye be true,
That is so vex'd with watching and with tears?
No marvel then, though I mistake my view;
The sun itself sees not, till heaven clears.
  O cunning Love, with tears thou keep'st me blind,
  Lest eyes well-seeing thy foul faults should find.

[CXLVIII]

150

My love is as a fever, longing still
For that which longer nurseth the disease;
Feeding on that which doth preserve the ill,
The uncertain sickly appetite to please.
My reason, the physician to my love,   †
Angry that his prescriptions are not kept,
Hath left me, and I desperate now approve
Desire is death, which physic did except.
Past cure I am, now reason is past care,   †
And frantic-mad with evermore unrest;
My thoughts and my discourse as madmen's are,
At random from the truth vainly express'd;
  For I have sworn thee fair, and thought thee bright,
  Who art as black as hell, as dark as night.   †

[CXLVII]

151

O, from what power hast thou this powerful might,
With insufficiency my heart to sway,
To make me give the lie to my true sight,
And swear that brightness doth not grace the day?
Whence hast thou this becoming of things ill,   †
That in the very refuse of thy deeds
There is such strength and warrantise of skill,
That in my mind thy worst all best exceeds?
Who taught thee how to make me love thee more,
The more I hear and see just cause of hate?
O, though I love what others do abhor,
With others thou shouldst not abhor my state:
   If thy unworthiness rais'd love in me,
   More worthy I to be belov'd of thee.

[CL]

152

The expense of spirit in a waste of shame
Is lust in action, and till action, lust
Is perjur'd, murderous, bloody, full of blame,
Savage, extreme, rude, cruel, not to trust,
Enjoy'd no sooner but despised straight,
Past reason hunted, and no sooner had,
Past reason hated, as a swallowed bait,
On purpose laid to make the taker mad:
Mad in pursuit, and in possession so,
Had, having, and in quest to have, extreme,
A bliss in proof, and prov'd, a very woe,
Before, a joy propos'd, behind, a dream;
   All this the world well knows, yet none knows well
   To shun the heaven that leads men to this hell.

[CXXIX]

153

Two loves I have of comfort and despair,
Which like two spirits do suggest me still:
The better angel is a man right fair,
The worser spirit a woman colour'd ill.
To win me soon to hell, my female evil
Tempteth my better angel from my side,
And would corrupt my saint to be a devil,
Wooing his purity with her foul pride.
And whether that my angel be turn'd fiend
Suspect I may, yet not directly tell;
But being both from me, both to each friend,
I guess one angel in another's hell:
     Yet this shall I ne'er know, but live in doubt,
     Till my bad angel fire my good one out.

[CXLIV]

154

Poor soul, the centre of my sinful earth,   †
. . . these rebel powers that thee array,   †
Why dost thou pine within and suffer dearth,
Painting thy outward walls so costly gay?
Why so large cost, having so short a lease,
Dost thou upon thy fading mansion spend?
Shall worms, inheritors of this excess,
Eat up thy charge? is this thy body's end?
Then, soul, live thou upon thy servant's loss,
And let that pine to aggravate thy store;
Buy terms divine in selling hours of dross;
Within be fed, without be rich no more:
     So shalt thou feed on Death, that feeds on men,
     And Death once dead, there's no more dying then.

[CXLVI]

Notes

As was indicated in the Preface, there is in the notes which follow very little attempt to explain difficulties by paraphrase. In the first place, though a poet may express himself obscurely in his own poetry, he cannot express himself at all in someone else's prose. And it seems to me that the reader who takes a short cut to the poet's 'meaning' by the aid of the 'condemned seconds' of an over-officious editor, instead of allowing his own understanding to follow the elusive meaning till he seizes it, runs the danger of having the meaning, for him, permanently weakened or distorted. For example, Malone writes a clear enough explanatory note: "They seem to mourn that those who are not born fair, are yet possessed of an artificial beauty, by which they pass for what they are not, and thus dishonour nature by their imperfect imitation and false pretensions." But that somewhat cumbrous prose is certainly not what Shakespeare wrote (and therefore not properly what he meant); he wrote:

> *and they mourners seem*
> *At such who, not born fair, no beauty lack,*
> *Slandering creation with a false esteem.*

In the second place, to comment on all the passages which present at least momentary difficulty would be to bury the text under commentary, apart from the fact that what is obscure to one reader may be as clear as daylight to another.

81

But it is perhaps permissible to comment on one or two general points of style which are observable in the sonnets, an awareness of which often accelerates comprehension. In the first place, while Shakespeare often writes a sonnet which is controlled by one particular image, at other times his metaphors shift with a bewildering and kaleidoscopic rapidity. As a result one has to be prepared to read different sonnets with quite different kinds of attention. Sometimes the only hope is to hold fast to the governing image and interpret everything in the light of it; at others the attempt to understand one line in the light of the image in its predecessor leads only to Cimmerian darkness. In the second place, an idiom which is not uncommon in the plays is almost a trick in the sonnets, a kind of transposition of adjective and noun; e.g. *old excuse, murderous shame, lovely argument, oblivious enmity*, mean 'excuse for age,' 'shameful murder,' 'theme of beauty,' 'injurious oblivion.' Thirdly, Shakespeare has a habit of almost violent compression, and this implies that the sonnets, if we are to extract their essence, must be read slowly, and without impatience; and above all we must, I think, be ready often to trust our 'feeling' for the meaning, and not try to arrive at it by grammatical dissection.

1. 7. *man in hue*; both *maiden* and *woman's* have been conjectured for *man in*, needlessly I think, since the point of the sonnet is that the subject of it combines the excellences of both sexes, and the shift from *woman* of ll. 1 and 3 is natural enough.

2. 10. *Richer than wealth, prouder than garments' cost*; cf. *Cymbeline*, III. iii. 23:

Richer than doing nothing for a bauble, (F Babe)
Prouder than rustling in unpaid-for silk.

3. *9. famoused for worth*; Q reads *worth* here, but *quite* in l. 11. We have to choose between *worth—forth* and *fight—quite*.

5. Through the sonnet runs a pun on 'shadow' (1) in its ordinary modern sense, (2) as a picture or symbol.

6. *7. for myself mine own worth do define . . .* ; various conjectures, e.g. *worth* to *define*, I do *all other . . .* ; *I myself my own worth* so *define*. But it is probably better to understand an 'I' before *do* from the *methinks* above. The whole two lines, however, are a trifle suspicious.

7. *4. expiate*; cf. *Richard III*, III. iii., *the hour of death is expiate*.

9. I suspect that these twelve lines of heroic couplet should not be included in the general run of the sonnets: they are generally taken as the envoy to the 'block' of sonnets that in Q ends with CXXV.

9. *2. fickle glass . . .* ; a wealth of conjecture. I fancy that the confusion is beyond cure and that *fickle* is no more than a misreading of *sickle* in the wrong place. We clearly have to retain in some shape the sickle and the hour-glass, but I see no compulsion to try to retain the jangling internal rhyme.

12. *10. Which this (Time's pencil or my pupil pen)*; so Q. The general sense is clear, that descendants would keep him alive in a way which no artist nor writer could achieve: and as the emendations, of which the easiest is *Which this time's pencil (or my pupil pen)*, do not much clarify the passage, I have left it as in Q.

13. *1. yourself*; it looks as though *yourself* must somehow mean 'your own.' One might perhaps emend to '*O that you ow'd yourself.*'

13. *13.* Punctuated as in Q, with no attempt to determine with which phrase *you know* should be taken—probably with both, as not uncommonly in Shakespeare.

15. 12. *mak'st waste in niggarding*; cf. *Romeo and Juliet*, I. i., *and in that sparing makes huge waste*.

16. 2. *trenches*; i.e. wrinkles, as in *Titus Andronicus*, V. ii., *Witness these trenches made by grief and care*.

19. 7. *beauteous roof to ruinate*; cf. 3 *Henry VI*, V. i., *I will not ruinate my father's house*.

20. 9. *from thine eyes my knowledge I derive*; cf. *Love's Labour's Lost*, IV. iii., *From women's eyes this doctrine I derive*.

20. 11. The inverted commas are Dowden's.

21. 12. *Nor it . . .* ; sc. 'There would remain,' or 'We should have.'

23. 8. *parts*; strictly one singer can only bear one part in a part song; but the meaning is clear enough, that by remaining single he prevents there being the concord of sweet sounds that there should be if he were married and had children.

23. 14. *Thou single wilt prove none*; cf. 131. 8, *Among a number one is reckon'd none*. There was a saying 'one is no number.'

24. 5, 6. Cf. *Measure for Measure*, I. iv., *her plenteous womb Expresseth his full tilth and husbandry*.

25. 12. *stretched metre*; a clear instance of a figure of speech very common in the sonnets (see general introductory note); it does not mean that the metre is strained, but that strained conceits are expressed in metre.

26. 4. *sable curls all silver'd*; cf. *Hamlet*, I. ii., *A sable silver'd*.

27. 5. *steep-up*; no hyphen in Q. But we have *steep-up hill* in *The Passionate Pilgrim*, and *steep-down gulfs* in *Othello*, V. ii. And perhaps in *Love's Labour's Lost*, IV. i., we should read *steep-up rising* instead of *steep uprising*, which is the usual division of Q's *steep up rising*.

27. 10. *reeleth from the day*; cf. *Romeo and Juliet*,

II. iii., *darkness like a drunkard reels From forth day's path.*

28. 1. *steel'd*; so Q. Ordinarily emended to *stell'd* (*i.e.* 'installed,' 'placed'). But why?

34. 6. *duly*; so Q. Usually, and probably rightly, taken as *dully* (cf. 35. 2). But it will stand, and is consistent with ll. 7 and 8.

35. 11. *Shall neigh—no dull flesh—in . . .* ; Q reads *naigh noe dull flesh in.* This punctuation, due to Malone, seems to give adequate sense. Cf. the first line of the next sonnet. This and the next two sonnets are full of the idea of the four elements.

36. 11. *earth and water*; cf. *Henry V*, III. vii., *He is pure air and fire; and the dull elements of earth and water never appear in him.* And *Antony and Cleopatra*, V. ii., *I am fire and air; my other elements I give to baser life.*

38. 11. Cf. *Romeo and Juliet*, I. v., *It seems she hangs upon the cheek of night Like a rich jewel in an Ethiop's ear.*

41. 9. *I tell the day to please him thou art bright*; so Q, with no punctuation. We can choose between putting a comma after *day* or after *him.*

41. 14. *strength*; the usual emendation of Q's *length.*

43. 1. *fell arrest*; cf. *Hamlet*, V. ii., *this fell sergeant, Death, Is strict in his arrest.*

43. 11. *The coward conquest of a wretch's knife*; this seems too specific to be merely a phrase for 'ignoble death,' and it is hard to resist the feeling that there is an allusion to Marlowe's death.

46. 8. Cf. Christina Rossetti's sonnet; *Better by far you should forget and smile Than that you should remember and be sad.*

46. 10. *compounded am with clay*; cf. *2 Henry IV*, IV. v., *compound me with forgotten dust.*

49. 9. *striving to mend . . .* ; cf. *King John*, IV. ii.,

When workmen strive to do better than well They do
confound their skill in covetousness, and *King Lear,* I. iv.,
Striving to better, oft we mar what's well.

50. *14. Being fond on praise* . . . ; the attempts to
explain the last couplet all, I think, break down over these
words. As they stand they must mean 'Being fond of
praise'; but fondness for praise is hardly a curse, and any-
how the remark is quite out of key with the rest of the
sonnet, the whole point of which is that the only possible
praise is simply to describe him as he is. The sense re-
quired is surely that his beauty is disastrous to his praisers,
because being beyond praise he makes their praises feeble: and I think we may justly suspect corruption.

51. *3. Reserve their character with golden quill;* various troubles; should *their* be *your?* Does character mean
'personality' or 'writing'? Should we read *deserve* or *re-*
ceive for *reserve? Reserve* should probably mean 'preserve,' and I think the meaning is simply 'comments in
your praise, expressed in precious phrases, are charac-
tered with golden quill and so everlasting.'

52. *4. Making their tomb the womb wherein they*
grew; cf. *Romeo and Juliet,* II. iii., *The earth that's na-*
ture's mother is her tomb; What is her burying grave that
is her womb.

59. *6. heavy ignorance;* cf. *Othello,* II. i., *O heavy*
ignorance!

60. *13, 14. us'd* . . . *abus'd;* for the rhyme and the
sense of *abus'd* (i.e. 'used out of place') cf. *Love's La-*
bour's Lost, II. i. 227.

61. *14. I will not praise that purpose not to sell;* cf.
Love's Labour's Lost, IV. iii., *To things of sale a seller's*
praise belongs.

62. *6. woo'd of time; time* means (I suppose) 'the
times'; i.e. 'you are sought after by everyone.' This at

least is the ordinary explanation, but it seems to make the phrase slightly weak for its context.

63. *14. soil*; usually explained as 'solution.' 'Soil' as a verb can mean 'resolve'; the substantive is not elsewhere found in this sense. It is more natural, I think, to take it as 'blemish'; i.e. 'the fault that causes your odour not to match your show is that you grow common.' (Q reads *solye*, but that is probably no more than a transposition error for *soyle*.)

64. *6. dead seeing*; unless we emend *seeing* this must mean 'an appearance of beauty which (being only paint) is dead.'

64. *12. proud of many*; if this is right, it must mean 'though there are many in the past for her to be proud of, *now* she lives only . . .' One's instinct rather is that *proud* conceals some word meaning 'bereft of' (e.g. *'priu'd* or *poore*).

65. *8–14.* Cf. *Love's Labour's Lost*, V. ii., *Fair ladies mask'd are roses in their bud; Dismask'd, their damask sweet commixture shown, Are angels vailing clouds, or roses blown*; and *Midsummer Night's Dream*, I. i., *earthlier happy is the rose distill'd, Than that which withering on the virgin thorn Grows, lives, and dies, in single blessedness.*

66. *8. rest*; Steevens's probable, though not essential, conjecture for Q's *west*.

66. *12. region*; either, as in *Hamlet*, II. ii. (*the region kites*) 'of this region,' or, as in *Romeo and Juliet*, II. ii., and *Hamlet*, II. ii., 'the upper air.'

67. *12. cross*; Q reads *losse* here as well as in l. 10. Cf. 68, *10–12*.

70. *7, 8.* This is the punctuation of Q, which I can see no reason to desert, and much to retain. In most texts the only stop before the end of l. 8 is a semicolon after *praise*.

73. 5. *world-without-end hour*; cf. *Love's Labour's Lost*, V. ii., *A time, methinks, too short To make a world-without-end bargain in.*

75. 6. *The imprison'd absence of your liberty*; a typical instance of violent compression. The writer is imprisoned (i.e. cut off from the society of his friend) by the friend's absence, which is due to the friend's liberty of action.

75. 11. *To what you will*; no doubt the emendation *time: Do what you will* gives a neater balance. But there seems no adequate reason to desert both the punctuation and the reading of Q.

79. 5, 6. *Gentle thou art* . . . ; cf. 1 *Henry VI*, V. iii., *She's beautiful; and therefore to be woo'd: She is a woman; therefore to be won.*

79. 8. *he*; so Q. But Tyrwhitt's *she* is very probably the true reading.

79. 9. *seat*; cf. *Othello*, II. i., *I do suspect the lusty Moor Hath leap'd into my seat.*

81. 13. *Or call*; Q reads *As cal.*

83. 3, 4. Cf. *Love's Labour's Lost*, II. i., *Beauty is bought by judgement of the eye, Not utter'd by base sale of chapmen's tongues.*

86. 1. *Devouring time*; cf. *Love's Labour's Lost* I. i., *Cormorant devouring time.*

87. 5. *golden tresses . . . second head*; cf. *Merchant of Venice*, III. ii., *So are those crisped snaky golden locks . . . often known To be the dowry of a second head, The skull that bred them in the sepulchre.*

88. 4. *three summers' pride*; cf. *Romeo and Juliet*, I. ii., *Let two more summers wither in their pride.*

88. 10. *Steal from his figure, and no pace perceiv'd*; cf. *Othello*, IV. ii., *The fixed figure for the time of scorn To point his slow unmoving finger at.* (Q reading.)

89. *1. forward violet*; cf. *Hamlet*, I. iii., *A violet in the youth of primy nature, Forward, not permanent.*

90. *3.* It looks as though Shakespeare was sending to his friend a note-book wholly blank or perhaps with this sonnet of presentation on its first page.

90. *10. blanks*; Q, *blacks.*

97. *5. The mortal moon hath her eclipse endur'd*; either 'Queen Elizabeth has died' or 'my love has come safely through a period of eclipse.' The whole tone of the sonnet depends on which interpretation we prefer.

99. Cf. for the idea of the sonnet the description of Rosalind as including in herself all the best qualities of the famous women of old, *As You Like It*, III. ii.

99. *12. They had not still enough your worth to sing*; so Q. *Still* is frequently emended to *skill*, but this surely, as Wyndham saw, gets the sense exactly wrong, missing the contrast with the last two lines. The old poets had the skill, but not the subject; we have the subject, but not the skill.

101. *3. what now to register*; so Q. Malone emended to *new*. Readers who agree that *new* 'gives the pleasure and the emphasis of repetition' will accept the emendation (which is probable enough); those who prefer the pleasure and emphasis of variety will retain the reading of Q.

102. There is a close resemblance between this sonnet and the dedication (to Southampton) of *The Rape of Lucrece*. Whether the resemblance is closer than we would expect to find between any two adulatory addresses is a matter of opinion.

103. *6. right*; so Q. We should perhaps read *rite*.

103. *9. books*; as *books* are not naturally thought of as *dumb* we should probably read *looks*.

105. *14. My most true mind thus maketh mine untrue*; neither emendations nor explanations are particu-

larly convincing. Malone conjectured *makes mine eye untrue*, which gives excellent sense (*true* meaning 'loyal to love,' and *untrue* 'fallacious'), but is not easy graphically. And both this and the explanations of the Q reading involve a sudden change of subject, from the eye with the vagaries of which the rest of the sonnet has been occupied, to the mind. I suggest as just possible, though awkward, that *mind* is not subject but object, and that the subject is still the eye, which turns the true (loyal) mind into an untrue (deceived) mind.

106. 4. *alchemy*; cf. *Julius Cæsar*, I. iii., *that which would appear offence in us His countenance, like richest alchemy, Will change to virtue.*

107. An admittedly difficult sonnet, over which the commentators tear their hair without arriving at any agreement. Being in no better case, I will only venture on a few suggestions: first, that *just* means 'true' (not 'morally right') and that ll. 3, 4 are an over-compressed way of saying that we lose the pleasure which for us is genuine when we estimate pleasure by others' judgment, not our own; second, that *give salutation to* may mean 'greet as an equal' and so 'stand on a par with'; and thirdly, that in l. 13 *they* may be not *all men*, but *they that level* of l. 9, and that l. 14 is a description of the *general evil*.

108. 10. *All frailties that besiege all kinds of blood*; cf. *Timon of Athens*, IV. iii., *Nature To whom all sores lay siege.*

110. 2. *love is not love . . .*; cf. *King Lear*, I. i., *Love's not love When it is mingled with regards that stand Aloof from the entire point.*

110. 8. *Whose worth's unknown . . .*; "Whose stellar influence is unknown, although his angular altitude has been determined" (Palgrave).

110. 9. *Time's fool*; cf. 1 *Henry IV*, V. iv., *But thought's the slave of life, and life Time's fool.*

110. 12. *bears it out even to the edge of doom*; cf. *All's Well*, III. iii., *We'll strive to bear it for your worthy sake To the extreme edge of hazard.*

111. 9. *that our night*; *that* is almost certainly not a conjunction, but demonstrative, and there seems no sufficient reason for changing *our* to either *sour* (Staunton) or *one* (Beeching).

112. 14. *besides methinks are dead*; so Steevens: Q reads *besides me thinkes y'are dead*, from which it is hard to extract any relevant sense.

117. 14. *Lilies that fester smell far worse than weeds*; the identical line occurs in *Edward III*, II. i.

121. 3. *made lame*; there is no sort of reason to take this, or 77. 3, literally. *Lame* is common enough in the figurative sense of 'disabled'; cf. *King Lear*, IV. vi., *A most poor man made lame by Fortune's blows.*

123. 7. *How have mine eyes out of their spheres been fitted*; cf. *Hamlet*, I. v., *Make thy two eyes, like stars, start from their spheres.* If *fitted* is the right reading it must presumably mean 'sent by fits.'

123. 10. *better is by evil* . . . ; the proverb which seems to be alluded to has not been identified, and the first *better* is somewhat suspicious; but any emendations are mere shots in the dark.

123. 14. *ills*; so Q; but l. 9 suggests that the singular may be the true reading.

125. 12. Cf. *Cymbeline*, II. iii., *Hark, hark! the lark at heaven's gate sings.*

126. 11. *upon misprision growing*; 'arising from a misapprehension'; cf. 1 *Henry IV*, I. iii., *misprision Is guilty of this fault.*

126. 13. *as a dream doth flatter*; cf. *Romeo and Ju-*

liet, V. i., *If I may trust the flattering truth of sleep, My dreams presage . . .*

129. The separation of this merely conventional exercise from its companion piece (147, CLIII) is a weakness of the 'Bray order.' Most readers will feel that neither has any business in the series at all.

131. 8. *one is reckon'd none*; cf. 23. 14.

132. 13. *Let no unkind, no fair beseechers*; so Q. If it is to stand, *unkind* probably means 'unkindness.' Dowden's conjecture is brilliant, *Let no unkind 'no' fair beseechers kill.*

136. 13. *more perjur'd I*; Q reads *eye*, which is perhaps right, as in any case there is a pun on 'I' and 'eye.'

139. 8. *Doth . . .* ; does this use of *doth* as 'confers' throw any light on the famous crux in *Hamlet*, I. iv., *Doth all the noble substance of a doubt?*

139. 9. *morning*; so Q. It matters little whether we read this, or *mourning* with most editors, since a pun is intended.

140. Cf. all the eulogies on dark beauty in *Love's Labour's Lost*, notably IV. iii.

140. 9. *eyes*; the word can hardly be right both here and in the next line; *raven* rather suggests that we should here read something meaning 'hair.'

143. 9, 10. *several . . . common*; cf. *Love's Labour's Lost*, II. i., *My lips are no common, though several they be.*

144. This sonnet appears, with certain variants, as the first poem in *The Passionate Pilgrim*.

148. 5. *roses damask'd, red and white*; 'damasked,' as well as meaning 'with the colour of the damask rose,' i.e. 'a fine deepe blush colour,' meant 'variegated,' cf. *Love's Labour's Lost*, V. ii., *their damask sweet commixture shown.*

149. 8. *Love's eye is not so true as all men's: no,
How can it*; this punctuation of Q is usually held up to
admiration as a marvel of subtlety. I believe that Lettsom
was right, that it was a mere blunder, and that we should
read *Love's eye is not so true as all men's 'no,'* with a pun
on 'eye' and 'ay.' Mr. Knox Pooler notes: 'It would seem
a pity to exchange for a pun one of the loveliest rhythms
in Shakespeare': but we have it on high authority that
Shakespeare himself would probably have felt such an
exchange far from a pity; and further, I feel (though this
is a matter merely of the individual ear) that Q's punctuation gives a rhythm lovely indeed, but utterly unlike the
Shakespeare of the Sonnets.

150. 5. *My reason, the physician to my love*; cf.
Merry Wives of Windsor, II. i., *though Love use Reason
for his physician* (if that emendation of *precisian* is accepted).

150. 9. *Past cure . . . past care*; the ordinary form of
the proverb is 'past cure, past care': Shakespeare here
seems to be saying the converse ('reason is past caring
for me, and so I am past cure'), and it is notable that
Love's Labour's Lost, V. ii. (both Q and F, though almost
universally transposed by editors) gives it in the same
shape, *past care is still past cure*. (But perhaps the easiest
interpretation, though it misses the reference to *reason*
in l. 5, is to take *reason is* as a parenthesis; see Glossary.)

150. 14. *black as hell, as dark as night*; cf. *Love's
Labour's Lost*, IV. iii., *Black is the badge of hell, The
hue of dungeons and the School of night*.

151. 5. *becoming of things ill*; cf. *Antony and Cleopatra*, II. ii., *vilest things Become themselves in her*.

153. The second poem (with variants) in *The Passionate Pilgrim*.

154. *1. the centre of my sinful earth*; cf. *Romeo and Juliet*, II. i., *Turn back, dull earth, and find thy centre out.*

154. *2.* The line begins in Q with the last three words of the preceding line.

Glossary

MANY words and phrases in Shakespeare require glossing, not because they are in themselves unfamiliar, but for the opposite reason, that Shakespeare uses in their Elizabethan and unfamiliar sense a large number of words which seem so familiar that there is no incentive to look for them in the glossary. It is hoped that a glossary arranged as below will make it easy to see at a glance what words and phrases in any particular scene require elucidation. A number of phrases are glossed by what seems to be, in their context, the modern equivalent rather than by lexicographical glosses on the words which compose them.

1

7 HUE, colour *or perhaps in the older meaning of* shape

11 DEFEATED, defrauded

2

4 HORSE, *plural*

5 HUMOUR, mood

3

4 JOY, *verb*
THAT, what

9 PAINFUL, worn
14 REMOVE, depart

4

1 ENDEARED, made more precious
5 OBSEQUIOUS, to do with obsequies
7 INTEREST OF THE DEAD, due to the dead

10 TROPHIES, memorials over a grave
11 PARTS OF ME, rights in me (?)

5

8 TIRES, headdresses (*but? should be* tire=*attire*)

9 FOISON, plenty

6

6 ACCOUNT, value
10 CHOPP'D, chapped

13 FOR, as, instead of

7

2 OF ONE DATE, contemporaries
4 EXPIATE, conclude

13 PRESUME NOT ON, (?) have no expectations of

8

4 LEASE, *cf. 'new lease of life'*
DATE, span, duration
7 FAIR, beauty
8 UNTRIMM'D, stripped

10 OW'ST, ownest
12 GROW TO, become united with (*and so last as long as time*)

9

5 WRACK, ruin
12 QUIETUS, quittance

12 RENDER, give back

10

1, 2 SINCE BRASS . . . POWER, Since there is no brass nor . . . which is not subject to death

3 RAGE, violence
10 FROM, away from
12 SPOIL, ravage

11

2 HOLDS, *intr.* remains
8 OUT OF MEMORY, into oblivion
9 CONCEIT, thought

11 DEBATETH, battles WITH, together with (*not 'against'*)

12

6 UNSET, unsown
9 LINES OF LIFE, living features

11 FAIR, beauty
13 STILL, yet existing

13

6 DETERMINATION, ending

10 HUSBANDRY, (?) *a pun*

14

2 DEPART, leave *or* distribute
4 CONVERT, turn away
7 THE TIMES, the world
8 MAKE THE WORLD AWAY, make away with the world

9 STORE, (?) fertility
14 COPY, original (or *perhaps simply* design)

15

5 CONTRACTED, betrothed
6 SELF-SUBSTANTIAL, of its own substance

11 CONTENT, potentialities
14 BY THE GRAVE AND THEE, (?) by dying childless

16

4 WEED, garment
9 USE, (?) investment

11 SUM MY COUNT, make my audit
OLD EXCUSE, excuse for age

17

7 USE, invest (*'profitless' because you pay interest to yourself*)

18

4 MAKELESS, mateless

19

6 STICK, hesitate

SONNETS

20

5 FORTUNE TO BRIEF MINUTES TELL, foretell what will happen each minute
6 POINTING, appointing
8 OFT, frequent

8 PREDICT, prognostication
12 STORE, begetting children
CONVERT, turn
14 DATE, last day

21

2 GAZE, spectacle
4 UNFAIR, take beauty from

14 LEESE, lose

22

3 TREASURE, make rich
6 HAPPIES, makes happy

14 CONQUEST, victim

24

5 UNEAR'D, unploughed
9 GLASS, reflection
11 WINDOWS, *either* eyes (*cf.* '*they that look out of the windows be darkened*') *or metaphor for* your children

25

4 PARTS, excellencies

11 RAGE, transports

26

2 BRAVE, gallantly adorned
9 QUESTION MAKE, reflect on

14 BREED, children

27

2 UNDER, in the world below

12 TRACT, course

28

1 STEEL'D, engraved

4 PERSPECTIVE, when looked at through something (? *my eye*) *or* from the proper angle

29

2 CONQUEST OF THY SIGHT, the spoils, *i.e.* the sight of you

9 IMPANNELED, *i.e. as a jury*
10 QUEST, jury

30

1 TOOK, made

31

3 PEACE OF YOU, peace that you give

14 OR, either
ALL AWAY, all being away

32

4 FOR BLUNTING, for fear of blunting
SELDOM, rare

8 CAPTAIN, chief
CARCANET, necklace

35

1 SLOW OFFENCE, exasperating slowness

6 SWIFT EXTREMITY, extreme of swiftness
14 GO, walk

36

4 WHERE, to where

11 WROUGHT, composed

37

9 RECURED, restored to completeness

38

6 INTEND, make, pursue
10 SHADOW, image

14 FOR, because of

39

1 WINK, close the eyes
2 UNRESPECTED, unregarded
5 SHADOW, image

5 SHADOWS, darkness
6 SHADOW'S FORM, the form that casts the shadow

SONNETS

41

11 SWART, black | 12 TWIRE, peep

43

3 INTEREST, share

44

1 OR, either

45

3 JOLLITY, magnificence | 11 SIMPLICITY, stupidity

46

10 COMPOUNDED, mingled

47

7 RESERVE, preserve | 8 HEIGHT, achievement

48

10 UNTRUE, untruly

49

7 OVER-GOES, surpasses | 11 PASS, result

50

4 EXAMPLE, give instance of | 14 FOND ON, fond of

51

1 IN MANNERS, being polite | 4 FIL'D, polished (*exactly* 'limatus')

52

3 INHEARSE, coffin up

6 PITCH, the height of a falcon before stooping

53

10 SOUNDLESS, too deep to be sounded

54

2 HAD . . . THY . . . GRACE, received thy favour

5 THY LOVELY ARGUMENT, theme of thy beauty

55

7 PENCIL, brush

7 LAY, apply

56

2 FAIR, beauty
4 TENDER, offer

5 SLEPT IN YOUR REPORT, idled in praising you
7 MODERN, ordinary

57

2 SHOW, appear

8 DIFFERENCE, variety

58

6 STAND AGAINST THY SIGHT, come before your eyes

13 CURIOUS, fastidious

59

3 AS, that
5 ON HIGH, aloud

13 ADVANCE, raise

60

2 O'ERLOOK, read
3 DEDICATED WORDS, words of dedication
5 HUE, form *or* colour

8 TIME-BETTERING, growing better by time
11 SYMPATHIZ'D, represented

SONNETS

61

4 REHEARSE, catalogue
5 MAKING A COUPLEMENT OF PROUD COMPARE, joining in flattering comparisons

8 RONDURE, sphere
13 LIKE OF, like

62

5 SO THOU BE, provided that you are
8 PRIME, youth

10 CHARG'D, assailed
12 TO, as to
14 OWE, possess

64

4 LACE, adorn

8 ROSES OF SHADOW, counterfeit of colour

65

5 CANKER-BLOOMS, dog-rose flowers
8 DISCLOSES, opens

10 UNRESPECTED, unregarded
14 VADE, fade
DISTILLS, *intr.*

66

6 RACK, cloud-mass
8 DISGRACE, disfigurement

14 STAIN, *intr.*

67

4 BRAVERY, splendour
ROTTEN, causing disease

8 DISGRACE, scar

68

8 APPROVE, test (*cf. 'on approval'*)

71

8 TRANSLATED, transformed

10 LIKE A LAMB, into the semblance of a lamb

72

8 HUMOUR, mood

73

10 SUPPOSE, conjecture

75

5 BECK, call

7 TAME TO SUFFERANCE, tame to the limit of endurance

9 CHARTER, licence

12 SELF-DOING, done by yourself

76

1 SET LIGHT, value lightly

2 PLACE IN THE EYE OF SCORN, look scornfully on

7 WHEREIN I AM ATTAINTED, with which I am tainted

77

3 LAMENESS, disability

6 SET A FORM UPON, justify, give a respectable colour to

78

6 AUTHORIZING, justifying

6 COMPARE, parallel instances

80

5 REMOV'D, of absence

81

6 WINK, close

8 DULNESS, drowsiness

10 NEW, *adv.*

82

2 PROUD-PIED, splendid in many colours

14 SHADOW, image

83

3 MERCHANDIZ'D, debased to the level of merchandize
ESTEEMING, value
7 FRONT, early days

11 WILD MUSIC, the songs of all birds
14 DULL, weary

84

3 FURY, transports (*cf. 'rage'* in 25)
6 GENTLE, noble

9 RESTY, sluggish
11 BE A SATIRE TO, satirise
12 SPOILS, ravages

85

1 AGAINST, against the time when

5 STEEPY, (?) o'er-towering, difficult of ascent (? *metaphor from course of the sun*)

86

11 UNTAINTED, *met. from tilting; a taint=a bit*

11 ALLOW, allow to be

87

1 MAP, detailed representation

3 BASTARD SIGNS OF FAIR, *i.e.* artificial aids to beauty

88

9 DIAL-HAND, hand from watch

10 FIGURE, *on a watch-face*

89

6 FOR, for theft from

90

6 MOUTHED, open-mouthed

10 BLANKS, blank leaves

91

1 TABLES, memorandum tab-
   lets
2 CHARACTER'D, written
3 IDLE RANK, trifling station
   (*i.e.* of tables)
7 RAZ'D OBLIVION, oblivion
   which razes

8 RECORD, memory
   MISS'D, lost
9 RETENTION, power of memory
10 TALLIES, tally, stick on
   which score was notched
14 IMPORT, argue

92

1 BEAR THE CANOPY, honour
   (*as by carrying canopy
   over*)
2 EXTERN, outward act

2 THE OUTWARD, *sc.* 'rank,'
   'magnificence'
11 SECONDS, second kind of
   flour

93

1 PRIDE, adornment
6 NOTED WEED, well-known
   garment

10 ARGUMENT, theme

94

4 DRESSINGS, refashioning
5 DATES, periods of existence

5 ADMIRE, wonder at
7 MAKE, think

95

8 ALTERING, *intr.*

96

1 STATE, circumstance *or* high
   estate
2 FOR, as being

9 POLICY, worldly wisdom
11 HUGELY POLITIC, (?) wise in
   large issues

97

3 LEASE, *almost* duration
4 CONFIN'D DOOM, fixed date

10 SUBSCRIBES, submits
14 CRESTS, device on a coronet

98

3 THESE CONTENTS, what is here (*in my poems*) contained

12 THE ENDING DOOM, final doomsday
13 THAT, when

99

1 WASTED, past
2 WIGHTS, creatures
5 BLAZON, praise, *or simply* description

8 MASTER, are master (owner) of

100

5 RECORD, remembrance
8 CHARACTER, writing
DONE, expressed

10 COMPOSED WONDER, miraculous composition
11 WHE'ER, whether *as monosyllable* (*often 'where' in Qq.*)

101

9 IN LOVE'S FRESH CASE, in a new instance of it

102

7 GOOD CONCEIT, favourable opinion

8 BESTOW, lodge (or ? clothe)
14 PROVE, test

103

2 PUT BESIDES, caused to forget

5 FOR FEAR OF TRUST, fearing to trust myself (?)
10 PRESAGERS, indicators

104

3 WHEN AS, when
CAST HIS UTMOST SUM, cast up his last account
4 ADVIS'D RESPECTS, deliberate consideration

10 DESERT, *i.e. lack of* deserving
14 WHY TO LOVE, why you should love

105

2 GOVERNS ME TO GO ABOUT, controls my movements
3 PART, abandon *or* divide
4 EFFECTUALLY, in fact

6 LATCH, seize
7 HIS, its
OBJECTS, *i.e.* the things 'latched'

106

5 INDIGEST, shapeless
11 GUST, taste

14 MINE EYE . . . DOTH FIRST BEGIN, *i.e.* is the king's 'taster'

107

9 LEVEL, take aim at
11 BEVEL, *the exact opposite of 'on the level'*

12 RANK, corrupt
13 GENERAL, universal
14 REIGN, persist (?)

108

2 QUALIFY, cool
7 JUST, punctual
WITH THE TIME EXCHANG'D, changing with time

12 FOR NOTHING, for the sake of nothing

109

6 TIME, the world

11 BRING . . . WITHIN THE LEVEL, 'bring your sights to bear on'

110

4 BENDS WITH THE REMOVER TO REMOVE, swerves when one of the two is false

9 FOOL, plaything
12 BEARS IT OUT, holds on

111

9 REMEMBER'D, reminded

12 HUMBLE SALVE, the salve of humility (*i.e.* apology)

SONNETS

112

1 FILL, *i.e.* conceal

8 STEEL'D, armoured (*with aes triplex*)

113

1 WITH MANNERS, becomingly

114

5 RESPECT, mutual relation
6 SEPARABLE SPITE, separating

9 I MAY NOT EVERMORE, I must for ever not . . .

115

4 DROP IN, *almost the modern colloquial sense*

8 LINGER OUT, drag out

116

4 NEW, *adv.*
6 DATELESS, eternal

8 EXPENSE, loss

117

2 SHOW, seem to do

5 RIGHTLY DO INHERIT, *probably not* deservedly are heirs of, *but* own and use rightly

118

10 EISEL, vinegar (*supposed prophylactic against plague*)

14 THAT, *demonst.*

119

4 FORWARDS, *adv.*
5 MAIN OF LIGHT, full light (*or possibly* ocean of light)
7 CROOKED, malignant

10 PARALLELS, trenches, *i.e.* wrinkles
13 TIMES IN HOPE, future times (?)

120

4 MORTAL, deadly
9 STATE, condition

10 STATE, magnificence

121

3 MADE LAME, disabled
  DEAREST, keenest
4 OF, from

8 THIS STORE, *i.e. your qualities*

122

2 MOTLEY, professional jester
3 GOR'D, wounded
4 MADE OLD OFFENCES, offended old friends
7 BLENCHES, side-glances

8 WORSE ESSAYS, experiments that failed
9 HAVE, *imperative*
10 GRIND, whet

123

2 LIMBECKS, stills (alembics)

4 SAW, 'fancied'

124

2 EAGER, tart
3 PREVENT, ward off in advance

11 TO MEDICINE, to the doctor
12 RANK, too full of

126

2 ESTIMATE, worth
3 CHARTER OF THY WORTH, freedom to which your worth entitles you

4 DETERMINATE, expired
8 PATENT, privilege

128

5 JACKS, keys of the virginal

130

1 CONSCIENCE, sense of right and wrong
2 CONSCIENCE, knowledge, perception

3 AMISS, fault
10 TRIUMPHANT PRIZE, prize of triumph

131

7 RECEIPT, power of receiving | 9 UNTOLD, unreckoned

133

8 PRIZING, troubling about

134

3 THAT OTHER MINE, my other self
9 STATUTE, security

11 CAME, who came
12 MY, *i.e.* that I suffer

135

6 ENGROSSED, monopolised

136

7 MISUSE, misrepresent | 11 GAVE, surrendered

137

13 WHAT THOU DOST HIDE, *i.e.* pity

138

11 ILL-WRESTING, twisting everything to the worst interpretation

139

8 DOTH, gives | 12 SUIT, fit *or* dress

140

3 SUCCESSIVE, next in succession | 6 FAIRING, beautifying

141

1 SO AS THOU ART, just as you are
11 ON ANOTHER'S NECK, 'on the head of' the last

142

11 WHO, which (*i.e. the heart*)

143

9 SEVERAL, private

144

11 HABIT, garb

145

4 ART, trickery (*cf. l. 7*)

146

2 PARTAKE, take sides

147

6 DATELESS, eternal

148

11 GO, walk
14 SHE, *substantive*

14 COMPARE, comparisons

149

4 CENSURES, judges

7 DENOTE, make clear, prove

150

6 PRESCRIPTIONS, instructions
7 APPROVE, prove the truth of
8 EXCEPT, reject

9 REASON IS, (?) reasonably
enough (*parenthesis*).
But see note
12 FROM, far from

151

2 WITH INSUFFICIENCY, deficient though you are

7 WARRANTISE, guarantee

113

SONNETS

152

1 WASTE OF SHAME, shameful
  wastefulness

153

2 SUGGEST, sway

154

8 CHARGE, expenditure
10 PINE, dwindle

10 AGGRAVATE, increase
11 TERMS, periods